Death Is No Dead End

Death Is No Dead End

By

BETTY RUTH SALLS

MOODY PRESS

CHICAGO

TO
the members of
Trinity Presbyterian Church,
Miami, Florida.
Through their prayers
and their ministry,
they wrote the book;
I just recorded
the happenings.

Contents

1

We Prayed, Believing

THE SPIRIT OF GOD moves mysteriously in your life and mine. What's up ahead? The most carefully laid plans can be torn asunder in one swift stroke.

I remember struggling over my annual pledge card a few years ago. *Lord,* I thought then, *if there were just some way to pay all my bills and get a few thousand dollars ahead, I could give and serve without reservation.* This train of thought seems so shallow now, and so long ago. I can see that *daily living* and *things* had a stronger hold on me than Christian service or dedication to God.

It only took a few short weeks for Him to show me what is most important. "Seek ye first the kingdom of God" was not a part of my philosophy. Most of my time was taken up in work and household duties.

Yes, I worked in the church, when I could. I helped my fellowman sometimes. But it took a tragedy—the death of my husband—to show me that I can cast all my cares, everything, on Him. He returned them to me, but not neatly worked out and tied up in gift wrappings according to my own will. His way involved pain and suffering such as I have never known, yet I could clearly feel that He had a plan. He entered my life in a new way.

Even as the waves of grief engulfed me, I began to feel His guidance. It always had been easy for me to ignore God's

9

nudgings. I paid very little attention to the plan that He had for me. Eight years ago I felt a call to write. This was a definite leading, conceived in prayer. It was so definite that I sold the first thing I wrote the first time it was sent out.

But I doubted, "Me, Lord? I have no training. I don't even know anyone who writes."

Yet I discovered that God is not limited by my weaknesses. He is most able when I am most incapable. The shock of Lawrence's illness would have been more than I could bear without His constant presence.

In the summer of 1969, our surgeon emerged from the operating room and told me that Lawrence had cancer of the pancreas. His chance for survival was 10 to 15 percent.

My husband was only forty-five. From outward appearances he was a strong, healthy man. We had been married twenty-five years, and I had never served him a meal in bed nor seen him in a hospital. He hadn't missed five days from work for illness in the past fifteen years.

Yet, in a very short time, every plan we had made together was changed. Intellectually, I suppose we believed in death, or else we wouldn't have had insurance. Emotionally, I didn't believe for one minute that God would allow my husband to die at his age.

Weren't we Christians? Didn't we believe in prayer? Doesn't the Bible say "Ask, and it shall be given you"; "If ye have faith as a grain of mustard seed, . . . nothing shall be impossible unto you"; "All things whatsoever ye shall ask in prayer, believing, ye shall receive"?*

If it was God's will for Lawrence to live, all he needed was one chance. I thought this would be one of God's miracles, and I looked forward to the time when he would be well. Surely his walk through the valley of the shadow of death would make him a stronger, more vocal Christian.

*Matthew 7:7; 17:20; 21:22.

The first small warnings of his illness appeared slowly. There was nothing to indicate that we should be seriously concerned. He began to feel tired just before we left on vation. Refusing to see a doctor, he ignored the symptoms. Hot weather, middle age—these were blamed for his condition. After a week in the mountains his skin turned yellow.

He still wasn't feeling sick. He had just finished building a porch on the cabin when I finally convinced him that he had to see a doctor. He wouldn't have done it then, except at that moment we were in a parking lot just outside a doctor's office. I was trying to get him to go inside, and he realized that I was going to burst out crying right there if he didn't.

The whites of his eyes revealed the same eerie shade of yellow as his skin. The doctor diagnosed it as hepatitis and ordered him into isolation at a hospital seventeen miles away. Lawrence even drove himself to the hospital. It was the last day he sat behind the wheel of a car.

He was treated for hepatitis for almost a week, and I was glad things had worked out so well. For a sick man, he felt very good. He had plenty of sick leave, and it appeared that we would just have an extended vacation while he convalesced here in this gorgeous section of the Blue Ridge Mountains.

When Lawrence was hospitalized, three of our five daughters were in the mountains with us. None of the girls were allowed to visit their Dad, so there wasn't much they could do by staying. Two days after he entered the hospital, Penny, our oldest, flew to her home in Indiana. Jeannie, our youngest, went with her. Bonnie, our twenty-one-year old, had just boarded a bus for a Bible conference in Montreat, North Carolina, when the blow fell.

Lawrence had to fly home for surgery! Eight hundred

miles! I had never driven the car for more than two hours at a time, and he had to fly home. At first he refused when I told him he was going by plane, but the reservation was already made. A neighbor called Penny to ask her to get Jeannie to the Atlanta airport by morning; I needed someone to ride home with me. Before we left the hospital, Lawrence insisted that I call Penny back to be sure Jeannie would be at the airport. Not only Jeannie was on her way, but Penny and her husband, Art, as well. I don't think Lawrence would have gotten on the plane and let me drive home by myself. But the three of them arrived just a half hour after he was airborne. I was never so glad to see anyone in my life!

Art drove all night, and we arrived at the hospital in Miami Sunday noon. The surgeon already had examined Lawrence and scheduled the operation for Wednesday morning. The yellow condition of his skin was caused by gallstones or an obstructive tumor.

A little voice inside me kept saying that Lawrence didn't have enough pain for gallstones. Just the same I prayed as I had never prayed for anything before, that this would be the diagnosis.

On Wednesday he was in good spirits, completely unafraid of the operation. When the doctor emerged from the operating room, our hopes were dashed. There was a malignant tumor at the head of the pancreas—cancer in its worst form.

We live in suburban Miami, where supposedly no one knows anyone else. But the news soon spread. By the time Lawrence came back from recovery, the hall outside his room was filled with people.

He looked twenty years older than when the stretcher had taken him away that morning.

That night we all began to pray in earnest. When we called Bonnie in North Carolina, her group began to pray. By 7:30

he was on several lists for Wednesday-night prayer meetings. Within the next few weeks we received word from far and near: "We're praying for you." A Catholic convent in Philadelphia kept him in their prayers. Lawrence's aunt, the wife of a Baptist minister in California, knelt in prayer for him twice a day. The Midwest, Canada, Africa, Viet Nam, the Blue Ridge Mountains—in all these places and more, people raised their voices claiming God's promises: "If ye have faith as a grain of mustard seed, . . . nothing shall be impossible unto you"; and "Whatsoever ye shall ask in prayer, believing, ye shall receive." It was part of our life. I believe the Bible literally. My God had all the power He needed to make Lawrence well. I prayed, convinced that he would be cured. Lawrence refused a private nurse. The girls and I stayed with him twenty-four hours a day. I slept in a chair at the foot of his bed. There are no words to describe my agony as I watched him suffer. His postoperative pain was worse than anything I have ever endured. Still, it never occurred to me that he wouldn't live.

In three weeks he was released from the hospital. He was to go home for two weeks and then return for the next operation—removal of the pancreas and malignancy.

These were two wonderful weeks. The doctor had told him that he had a tumor, but not that it was malignant. By now he had a large scrapbook of letters and cards, prayers and poems that people had sent to him. Everything was in his favor. He was strong, vigorous, and young for this type of surgery. Our surgeons were the best. The hospital had all the modern equipment. Everyone we knew was praying. With all that, how could he lose?

And yet, even as I prayed, a small voice within me kept saying, *But just think of what Christ suffered. He was God's only begotten Son. He prayed all night in the garden. Yet*

He died on the cross, beaten and abused, with no one to give Him comfort in His last hours.

Maybe—just maybe—the God who had sacrificed His own Son, wouldn't spare Lawrence's life either. I closed my eyes and my mind, and I shut out the awful thought. Surely *my* husband would not die, no matter how small his chances were.

The day of the operation arrived. It was Bonnie's birthday, and the day before my own birthday. I arose at two in the morning, had a cup of tea, knelt by my bed, and prayed that my husband would be healed. Then I asked that we would have strength for anything that was in store for us. In those early hours He took my burden upon Him. I left my burden with the Lord and went to the hospital.

Lawrence already was up and shaving. His outlook was wonderful. He planned to be back at work in no more than four weeks. At seven o'clock four of our daughters arrived. He teased them and they teased him, and he danced a jig to make them laugh. At 7:45 the stretcher came. We kissed him outside the surgery door. As soon as he was inside, we went to the cafeteria to eat breakfast, knowing he would be all right for the next half-hour. I didn't leave the surgical floor again for almost forty-eight hours.

2

The Lord Said No

HOUR AFTER HOUR we sat in the tiny room just outside surgery. The girls became restless and I sent them home for a while. About two o'clock that afternoon the surgeons appeared at the door. The lines in their faces were deeper. Their eyes revealed the weariness of a long, hard battle; but they were optimistic. They felt that they had removed all of the cancer and that Lawrence had as good a chance for survival as anyone who had undergone intensive surgery.

I waited two more hours and the stretcher appeared in the hall. I walked beside it to the door of the intensive care unit. Lawrence was awake and knew me, but he was in pain. However, his color was good and my hopes were high as the door closed behind him.

The small waiting room for the intensive care families was crowded. Four patients besides Lawrence were inside. I joined the others in their all-night vigil and slept on a blanket on the floor. Every two hours we could be admitted to see the patients. Around ten o'clock I realized that all was not well; they were working frantically over him. The pacemaker was connected, and at times he was packed in ice. At 3:30 in the morning, it seemed to me that he had rallied. He was teasing the nurse about how mean she was when she told me it was time for me to leave. That was the last time I saw him when he was completely coherent. Through it all he was in terrible pain. Most of the time the next day the doctors were with him, and I wasn't allowed in. When I did go in, he was not awake. As the evening progressed he grew worse. At length I knew that he might not live through the night, and the doctor confirmed my fears.

I discouraged the girls from going to his bedside. Once Penny ventured inside the room. She was about two steps behind me. Out of the corner of my eye, I saw her clamp her hand over her mouth to stifle a scream and run from the room. She had been trained as a nurse's aide, and the pacemaker meant death to her. I let her go. There were enough people in the waiting room to help her. Nothing was important now except Lawrence. The younger girls did not want to see him in pain. He wasn't asking for them, so they waited outside.

By now, the nurses were letting me stay with him most of the time. They were still working to save his life, but they made a bargain with me. I could stay as long as I didn't get upset when they drew blood from his incision and performed other ghastly duties. The Lord was with me. I was determined not to interfere with their work, and He sustained me in this decision.

Around midnight, Lawrence aroused enough to ask for Barbara. He was semi-conscious and kept repeating, "Barbara, Barbara, Barbara."

Our twenty-year-old daughter was upstairs in another hospital bed, suffering from a serious infection that had not yet been diagnosed. He had seen her the night before the operation, but she was the only one who had not walked with him to the surgery door.

"Barbara is all right. She is getting better. Don't worry about her; she is going to be fine. Now I want you to get well." Over and over I told him this until it seemed to penetrate.

His next and last words were, "Pray, Betty; pray, Betty; pray, Betty."

I couldn't pray. I had left his fate with the Lord when I prayed in the wee hours of the morning before surgery. Now I was too miserable to pray. My minister was out of town, or he would have been with us.

As a nurse stepped up to the bed to check his intravenous solution, I opened the door and said to a friend, "Would you see if you can get Ray Davies, please?"

I saw my daughters begin to sob softly, and then my eyes fell on Dorothy Cleland. She was a minister's widow. When I first met her, her husband had suffered a heart attack and was forced to retire from a paid ministerial position. But he had never retired from spreading God's Word. At his death, Dorothy was an inspiration to everyone. Briefly, I remembered a portion of his funeral service. The minister had said, "This is not a funeral, but a coronation. Today Ronald Cleland lives with our King."

For a split second, I wondered how Dorothy knew to come here tonight. She said, "What can I do for you, Betty?"

Then I knew why she had come. God sent her here to pray when I couldn't.

Quickly I said, "Pray. Just pray." As she bowed her head, I closed the door and went back to Lawrence's bedside.

He never woke up again. Ray Davies, the minister from a neighboring Presbyterian church, was there within minutes.

Mr. Davies said, "He is fighting. He may make it. I believe that the Lord can save his life if it is His will." And he prayed. We talked for a while and he prayed again.

Then I sent him outside to be with the girls. I never gave up hope until the medical staff pronounced Lawrence dead.

His color was good, his cheeks were red, and he didn't look like a man who was going to die.

We prayed and the Lord said *no*. As I stood there beside his bed, an inner voice said, *I will not leave you comfortless.*° The emptiness inside me defied description. I knew Lawrence was dead. I saw him take his last breath. Yet it was impossible for me to grasp the reality. I simply did not want to be a widow.

My mind went back to the last time I had waited for death in this same hospital. My next-door neighbor, a lovely thirteen-year-old girl, had become ill while swimming. Lawrence and I had rushed her here, to the hospital. In the early hours of the morning she passed from life into death, and her family was without comfort.

The girls had to be told. I prayed for the "peace that passeth understanding," that when I stepped back into the waiting room I could control my emotions. I knew that if I became hysterical, the girls would, too.

No, God, don't let us disturb the sleeping patients on this hospital floor.

The voice within me said, *If you would find peace, do something for someone else.*

"His eyes," I wondered out loud, "could a sightless person see through them?"

Quietly, the nurse said, "Are you sure? Is this really what you want to do?"

"Yes, I'm sure. If he were blind, I'd want someone to do that for him."

As I made my decision, the peace of God which passes all understanding *did* settle within me; and I returned to the waiting room.

Linda and Jeannie, my two youngest daughters, were

°John 14:18.

asleep—Linda on the couch, and Jeannie wrapped in a blanket on the floor. No one needed to ask if Lawrence was gone. As I sat down to wait for the paper to sign to donate his eyes to the blind, the others began to move on stiff legs as if they were robots, picking up our belongings. Among other things were the birthday presents that had arrived for me all day in an effort to cheer me up. I couldn't help thinking, as I saw them packing the gifts into a bag, that the only thing I had wanted for my birthday was the thing I didn't get —Lawrence's life.

3

God Is There When We Need Him Most

AT LAST the entire group moved toward the elevator. Outside we separated into the four waiting cars and drove home through dark streets. It was 4 A.M.—a desolate, dark time to come to grips with a desolate, dark reality! I was a brand-new widow. Numbly, I sat in the car beside my sister, Jean, too stunned to think.

Strong coffee and daylight brought me to my senses. There were things to do, and the most important was to go back to the hospital about the time Barbara would wake up and tell her the horrible news. Vern, her fiance, had asked me to wait until he snatched a few hours sleep so he could go with me. It wasn't until he left that I remembered Barbara called early every morning to talk to me. If she called the intensive care waiting room and someone else told her, that would never do. I waited for Vern as long as I dared, then Jean drove me back to the hospital.

The worst part was that no one had told her that her dad was in critical condition. Her own condition was poor, but the first thing she asked as I entered the door was, "How's Daddy?"

Her hysterical sobs echoed throughout the west wing, and we soon were surrounded by nurses and aides. Vern arrived in the middle of the confusion and was a welcome sight. To hear Barbara screaming for her father was tearing me to pieces and was worse than watching him die. A hypo soon quieted her. Suddenly I felt stifled, completely appalled by the thought of sitting in the hospital another minute. I had to leave or I would be screaming too.

It couldn't have been more than eight o'clock when He began to send expressions of His love and the love of His people.

The first food that arrived was four pounds of cottage cheese! Grimly, I put it in the refrigerator beside the two pounds I already had; and I wondered, "What in the world will we do with six pounds of cottage cheese?"

But I was to learn that God had even taken into account my squeamish stomach. The cottage cheese was the only thing I could eat for several days. When I finally felt better, the six pounds of cottage cheese were gone. If it hadn't been there, I wouldn't have eaten anything. Certainly it would never have occurred to me to send out for six pounds of cottage cheese!

For the girls and the guests, there arrived dozens of dishes of tastefully prepared food. There were phone calls and telegrams and offers of help. Barbara's fiance stayed with her in the hospital from early morning until late at night so that one of us wouldn't have to sit with her. Our son-in-law arrived again from Indiana. Without a word, he mowed the lawn, serviced the cars, and chauffeured me back and forth to the hospital to see Barbara. He did everything Lawrence had been unable to do these past weeks. People who had worked with Lawrence, people I hardly knew, stopped by with food and comfort.

As I look back now, I realize that we weren't really in physical need. We could have managed without all the help and all the food. But each kindness was as a healing balm poured over us. Our sorrow was being washed away by love and concern. Until you have been through this experience, you cannot know the value of a dish of potato salad or fried chicken. I could hang my head in shame at the times I have stayed away from a house of bereavement because I didn't know just what to say, or because I didn't know the people especially well. Some who came from the church actually had to introduce themselves.

How much courage would it take to go to a grief-laden stranger and say, "What can I do?" That had been a lesson I had not wanted to learn, but my own bereavement taught me something about ministering to those in trouble.

The night after he died, I was comforted by a very unusual experience. All day I had avoided the bedroom because I couldn't look at his empty bed. That evening I had the bed removed and put in the family room so that Penny's father-in-law, who had been one of Lawrence's best friends, could sleep on it. It didn't help. The empty space was as upsetting to me as the bed had been. With never-ending patience, the boys next door moved a desk from the family room into my bedroom, then a chair, and then my typing table.

When I could think of nothing else to do to prolong the ordeal, I went into the master bathroom to prepare for bed. As I stepped from the tub, a severe chill settled in my bones and I began to shake. In bed, with a blanket and a heavy spread over me, my teeth still chattered. I couldn't turn off the air conditioner, because it helped cool the other bedrooms and the night was hot and humid. I got out of bed and rummaged through the dresser drawers for something warmer to sleep in. I found Lawrence's pajamas and returned to the bathroom away from the air conditioner to put them on. As I pulled them over my own clothes, the warmth they still held from being folded in the sunshine spread over me. I buttoned them up and glanced into the mirror. Directly behind me, just as he had stood for the past twenty-five years, was the reflection of my husband.

It was there for only a second; but he said to me, "You might as well go to bed and get a good night's sleep. You know you will have to do everything that we both would have done if I had lived. I can't help you anymore."

I've never been one to put my faith in communing with the spirits. It is impossible for me to explain this experience, except that God knows exactly what our needs are every moment and allowed me this brief vision to reassure me. Until I saw Lawrence's reflection and felt a Presence fill that bathroom, I was not absolutely sure that Lawrence had gone to heaven. He was a member of a church; he had accepted Christ; he had a changed life; and yet I could never understand why he was not more filled with the Holy Spirit. With two of our daughters, he attended the 8:30 morning service at our church as often as he was home. Then an elder called to ask if he would be willing to serve as a deacon. The very idea scared him half to death! He was an extremely shy person. He thought about it for three days. I begged him to accept the nomination. My sister and brother-in-law talked to him about it. Our children encouraged him to accept. Yet, he declined.

"Why?"

"Because I don't want to be a deacon," he said. Then, to make sure that he wasn't asked again, he attended church less and less.

"Do you believe in Christ?" I asked.

"Yes."

"That He died on the cross for you and rose again and only through Him can you go to heaven?"

"Yes."

"Then why don't you serve Him?"

"Because I don't want to be a deacon," he said.

His worship took more the form of Billy Graham Crusades on television, or Sunday church programs on radio or TV. When the Korean Orphans toured the US he got me out of bed to hear them sing hymns. But he would not serve as a deacon! I could see his life changing. There was a personality growth, but his initial shyness among strangers persisted.

Why? I thought. *Why doesn't Christ change this too, if he is truly a Christian?*

Once, after we learned he had cancer, I felt that he was awake in the middle of the night.

"Lawrence," I said, "if something happens and you don't recover from the next operation, are you sure that you are going to heaven?"

"Yes, I guess so. But nothing's going to happen."

Knowing Lawrence, I felt that this was all I would get out of him. If he said, "I guess so" or "probably," when you asked him anything, that was a maddening (to me) *yes.*

He often meant yes, even when he said no. Living with six women as he had all these years, he felt it was his prerogative to be begged to agree with us. Often he would tell me he didn't think the car would be ready for a planned weekend trip. We never missed a trip because of the car, but he always told me it wouldn't be ready on time.

Thus I accepted his *I guess so,* as yes. I didn't think that anything would happen either.

After he died it really bothered me when I realized that his *I guess so* could have been *no* in the eyes of God.

His Presence and Lawrence's reflection, I'm sure, were the answers to my question. Had he not gone to be with God, the warm feeling of Christ's love would not have been present when I saw the reflection.

Mulling this over, my chill subsided and I slept soundly all night. The next morning I awoke and reached for a small box of Bible verses which I kept by my bedside. The verse on top came alive to help me through the ordeal that I faced:

> But they that wait upon the LORD shall renew their strength; they shall mount up with wings as eagles; they shall run, and not be weary; and they shall walk, and not faint.
>
> ISAIAH 40:31

The days that followed were not easy, but they were easier because I had seen Lawrence again, alive and well. His old body had not held him in death. I knew that he had gone to be with God. And the Lord had promised me strength to run and not be weary, to walk and not faint. This was significant to me because, when both my parents died, I had become physically ill from nerves. I had actually fainted, had no strength, and was terribly weary. This time, waiting on the Lord made a world of difference.

When I went to select a casket, I thought I couldn't bear the strain of looking over the dreadful merchandise in that cold, forbidding room. Yet, even as the undertaker held the door for me to enter, I could hear Lawrence say, *Don't you waste my money. They aren't going to put me in that box. What's left is only an empty shell.*

With a minimum of effort, I selected an attractive, but inexpensive, casket and escaped the chilling depression that filled the room.

As the hours wore on while we were receiving friends in the funeral home, the strength and help that God had promised were evident. My nieces were crying so hard in the anteroom that I sent Linda out to comfort them, and she was able to do so. The poise and self-control displayed by all four of our daughters (Barbara was still in the hospital) as they greeted the mourners could only have been an act of God. For five hours people came and went in steady streams. I was gripped with a fear that I would not recognize some of them. Occasionally I didn't, as they entered the door. But by the time they crossed the room, their names would spring forth from the haziness of my mind and separate themselves from my other thoughts. I could make introductions with no apparent effort. Names often escape me completely, even under ordinary circumstances. That day it was just as if Someone were remembering through me.

As usual when I needed her, there was Dorothy Cleland. Discussing the large number of lovely floral arrangements, she said, "You know, when Ron died, I sent several of the smaller ones to shut-ins so they could enjoy them, instead of taking all of them to the cemetery."

I knew Lawrence would rather have the flowers sent to sick people than left to wither in the hot sun. His completely practical mind was my guide. I saved six of the smallest bouquets and delivered them myself the day after the funeral. It was the best therapy anyone could have prescribed. As I visited briefly in the homes of the shut-ins, my own needs and grief began to take on their proper proportions. It is *important* that you get your mind off yourself.

The funeral actually stands out in my memory as a time of enrichment. The church was filled; many came who never attend church. They were of all faiths and from many different circumstances. They came with different ideas and different ideals to pay tribute for the last time to Lawrence. The casket in the front of the church was meaningless to me because I knew Lawrence was walking with the Lord even as we gathered for the service.

Barbara was brought from the hospital in a wheelchair. She was so sick that it was truly God's help which enabled her to sit through the whole thing. For days she had fainted every time she got out of bed. Yet she insisted that she wanted to attend the funeral. On this day extra strength was necessary, and God supplied her needs.

It was a memorable experience—a real tribute to Lawrence as a husband, father, and Christian. The pastor spoke on the Twenty-third Psalm. "Yea, though I walk through the valley of the shadow of death, I will fear no evil: for thou art with me; thy rod and thy staff they comfort me. Thou preparest a table before me in the presence of mine enemies: thou anointest my head with oil; my cup runneth over. Surely goodness and mercy shall follow me all the days of my life: and *I will dwell in the house of the* Lord *forever."*

Then he went on to the gospel of John: "Let not your heart be troubled: ye believe in God, believe also in me. In my Father's house are many mansions: if it were not so, I would have told you. I go to prepare a place for you. And if I go and prepare a place for you, I will come again, and receive you unto myself; *that where I am, there ye may be also."**

Lawrence had gone to be with the Lord; and we were left with the words of Paul, "All things work together for good to them that love God, to them who are the called according to his purpose."***

Is there any good in the death of a young father? Can there be any purpose in this tragedy? I knew it was up to the Lord and me to make good come of it, or else Lawrence's life would have been in vain. The only visible marks that either of us had made in the world were five fine daughters. Could his death in some way have more meaning than his

*14:1-3; italics added.
**Romans 8:28.

life? Could *all things,* even death, work together for good?

When the funeral was over and the limousine drove away from our door, I heard one of the younger girls say, "Are we supposed to stay in these clothes all afternoon?"

Without any hesitation Penny made the decision for all of us. "Not the way Daddy hated black, we're not. We're going to change right now."

As I slipped out of the somber funeral dress, I could hear Lawrence say, "And don't put it on again."

We donned the bright colors of summer, and our world began to come into focus a little more. By the time we emerged from the bedrooms, the house again was filled with people bringing food and comfort.

The question hung heavily in our hearts and minds. *Why did he die?* Did God have something for him to do in heaven? Was it to test our faith as Job had been tested? Was it an accident? Maybe God had meant for him to live, but man has not yet found a cure for cancer! Every one had a suggestion, but no one had an answer.

Yet, the Bible is clear on this point: "*All things* work together for good to them that *love God,* to them who are the called according to His purpose." Could I believe that? Or would my faith wither and die?

4

A Different Life

A FUNERAL gives a finality to your life that nothing else can. First Lawrence's spirit had departed from the earth, and now his body was gone. There was not one more thing that I could do for him. Forty-seven days ago I had badgered him into seeing a doctor. In all of those days I had but one thought—we must do what was best for him. His health and welfare came first. Now he was gone and there was a tremendous void in my life.

But the Lord filled it.

Soon I began to realize that Lawrence no longer could do the many things he had always attended to for me and the girls. Outside in the driveway stood four cars that he had always kept in top-notch condition. I had never done anything to them but turn the key in the ignition. I had never called the garage, never bought a tire, and had no idea how often the oil should be changed. Until the funeral was over, I had grief only because we lost *him.* Now I was aware that we had lost more than a husband and father. We were separated from his love and laughter, and the twinkle in his eyes; but not until now, as we began to pick up the pieces of our daily life, did we realize that his salary was gone, his strength was gone, and his advice was gone. There were so many things I would have asked him if I had believed that he was going to die.

My first challenge came just a few hours after the funeral. As people began to depart, I asked Art, my son-in-law, to drive me to the hospital to see Barbara.

On the way he said, "What can we do for you?"

"Nothing. There's not a thing anyone can do."

"Well," he said, "we've been talking about moving to Miami so we would be close enough to help when you need it."

How I longed to say, "Oh goodie, why don't you do just that?"

But that still small voice inside said, *Oh no, that's not their responsibility.*

I found myself saying, "Not for me, you aren't going to move. I'll get along just fine without that."

"But how can you take care of four kids and four cars and the house without help?"

"I don't know, but I'll think of something. I see other women doing it, and I'm vaguely as smart as anyone else."

That afternoon I knew that, one by one, I would have to turn loose of my children. I wasn't left with babies; mine were young adults. In the course of a few years, I would be alone. In the back of my brain one line from a song was wandering around, "Let my people go."

My husband was gone, and the girls would be leaving soon. Could I take it all in my stride? I really didn't know how. I knew only that I must find a way; I could not let my grief and loneliness ruin other lives.

To help fill the chasm that was left in my life, the Lord gave me an unusual sense of responsibility to utilize to the best advantage all the things Lawrence did leave us. I realized that if I was going to do this, there was no time to sit around moping and mourning. I had no time to waste at all, and this is how Lawrence would have wanted it. Hadn't he danced a jig just twenty minutes before the stretcher took him to surgery, so we would laugh? The last thing in the world that he would want would be a house and a family full of gloom.

We had to live differently if we were to be successful in this new life.

One of the first things I had to face was the big tree in the yard that had to come down. Without Lawrence here to trim it, it would fall on the house during a high wind. Hurricanes often lurked a few hundred miles out in the Atlantic. Knowing this, I had tried to trim its longest branches just before his last operation. I intended to do it while he took his afternoon nap; however, he stepped out the door just in time to see me lose my balance and almost fall from the top of the pump shed.

"What are you doing? That is no work for you. Get down right now."

I did because I was afraid I really would fall. I didn't say a word to him; but as we sat in lawn chairs, I was thinking, "How am I going to get this tree trimmed?"

He knew what I was thinking. "You have no problem!" He grinned. "If you go visit a friend for a couple of hours, it will be done when you come back."

"I know, and that's exactly why I'm not going anywhere," I retorted.

His doctor's orders had been explicit. He could sit in a chair, ride in a car if I drove, and walk around a little bit. He knew this; and yet, if I had turned my back, he would have trimmed the tree.

That tree was almost a part of us. Lawrence and I drank coffee in the shade there every afternoon. It had been our "roof" for barbeques and fish fries and watermelon cuttings for years. Yet it must go because I couldn't trim it.

I rented a chain saw, and my cousin came to wield it. He cut and we carried, and at the end of the afternoon our favorite tree was stacked at the curbside awaiting the next day's trash pickup.

For a moment I looked at it and thought, *I just can't stand it. Am I going to have to get rid of everything I ever enjoyed?*

Then I reflected. It was a material thing and not important. To sacrifice the tree for the preservation of the house was the logical thing. After all, this was a new life; and Lawrence and I would never again drink coffee in the shade of that tree.

His workshop had to be cleaned. With a lot of misgivings I began by gathering up the scrap metal to take to a salvage dealer. Although I mentioned it to no one, I was afraid to go. In those days I was afraid to do everything, because I had never done anything. The junkyard was near the river in what could be a bad section of town. To my surprise, the burly, rough-looking workers were as polite and respectful to me as any businessman in my neighborhood. They paid me $15.00 for a trunkfull of junk that I almost put out for the garbage man.

The days when I received an insurance check or money from Lawrence's retirement fund were terrible. I was seized with a fear that I wouldn't take care of the money properly. Most of the checks were delivered by registered mail or an insurance agent. Even that upset me.

But one day, just after I had returned to work, the City of Miami insurance office phoned. I was to pick up the check at City Hall that afternoon. Immediately I was in a terrible emotional state. It seemed that I would never make it to City Hall unless someone went with me. But I was ashamed to ask because everyone had already done so much. My hard head would not let me ask anyone to go. However, God occasionally puts my stubborn disposition to good use.

After work I picked up Jeannie at school. To my surprise she insisted that she wanted to go with me.

It turned out to be all I needed. I had thought I could not even drive the car, but I did not want to let her know that I was upset. Pretty soon I felt fine. It was a good lesson for me. I was learning that the hardest part of all these added duties was thinking I couldn't do them. Once I had made up my mind to go ahead, half the battle was over.

As far as Lawrence's estate was concerned, he had none. Everything we owned was in both our names with a survivorship clause. Having heard alarming stories of legal entanglements and frozen bank accounts, I knew what a blessing this was.

The funeral director advised me to get numerous copies of the death certificate. I disliked the idea; and although I carried them in my purse for several weeks, I did not have the courage to look at them. One by one they were dispensed— to the mortgage company, to pay off a bank loan, to the county tax office for widow's exemption, to the Social Security office, to the Veterans' Administration. How I loathed those little black and white photostats, proof that I no longer had a husband.

One day my brother-in-law asked me something about the death certificate, and I handed it to him. "Hmmm," he said, "Lawrence had cancer for approximately one year."

As I was working on the accounts a few days later, it suddenly occurred to me that this was another proof that *God's hand had been in Lawrence's illness all the time.* Just a year before Lawrence died, an incident occurred that forced me to take out more insurance on all the family. I did it grudgingly, but this is the only reason that we are financially secure now.

Apparently I bought the insurance at about the same time the cancer began to grow in his body!

When I went to the Social Security office to apply for benefits for Linda and Jeannie, I didn't realize that I could apply for anything else. The gentleman in the office was most helpful. He explained to me that, if I could hold my income to $140 a month, I could receive Social Security benefits as a mother of minor children until Jeannie was eighteen years old. I had no interest in what he was saying. But he was so sure it was something I should think about, that he applied for my benefits anyway.

At first it seemed like a ridiculous thought. My practical brain kept telling me that I needed my job now more than ever. However, the Lord kept insisting that I could serve Him better if I quit working for a few years. I had been reasonably successful writing part time, and I longed to step out in faith to see if I could earn my living at it. The idea kept gnawing in my mind.

One day a friend asked me, "Betty, how can you keep going and retain your faith as you have in the face of this? You've never had an easy life—Barbara sick all the time, medical expenses to pay. You've worked for years to educate the girls, and now this. How can you stand it?"

I tried to explain to her that *now* was when I needed my faith most. This was certainly not the time to throw it away. God had been with us each step of the way. I could never have gone through this without Him. However, I was dissatisfied with my answer as it came out, and I began to feel that I could have more influence on people's lives if I wrote about my faith. Perhaps this was the answer since I was so tongue-tied when someone asked me about it.

For several weeks a tremendous tug-of-war was waged within me. Sometimes the Lord would win and I would decide to quit my job. Then my intellect would take over, and the Lord would be pushed into the background. Logic would tell me that "security" was the most important thing. Hadn't I worked for the school board for six years? Didn't they have every fringe benefit known to man?

"But there you can't think and write for Me, and I have lots of work for you," the Lord would insist from the corner of my mind where I had pushed Him.

Finally one day it happened. He won. I got out of my chair and walked over to the registrar's desk and said, "I quit."

5

Encouragement Comes from Everywhere

IF I EXPECTED opposition from my employers, I was mistaken. Everyone was with me all the way. My friends had more faith that I could write than I did. There have been many times when I've looked back and asked myself and the Lord if we knew what we were doing.

The reaction of people, when they learned that I had given up my job, was interesting to watch. One friend who has no faith in her own ability to do anything had all the faith in the world that I could write if I tried.

Dorthy Cleland was my biggest surprise. Shortly after the funeral, she brought me Catherine Marshall's book, *To Live Again.* It was one of the things that made me decide to quit my job and try my hand at writing.

I said to her, "Dorothy, the book you gave me to read was so inspirational that I have quit my job."

She was dumbfounded. Her first reaction was that I should have waited until I retired with a pension before daring to give up my income.

We were on our way to an Augsburg Crusade in the Dade County Auditorium. On the way back, she was telling me about seeing Oral Roberts on television, healing people through prayer and faith. Her eyes sparkled as she related each detail.

I said to her, "Dorothy Cleland, how can you believe *that* and still be afraid that the Lord is going to let me starve to death if I quit my job?"

She had more faith than anyone I knew, and yet she let it falter when she thought that my security was in danger. This is what I had done all my life. In my head, I believed that God was in command; that He would lead in every situation. But when action required taking a chance, going out on a limb, I wonder if He is there. Will He really take care of us? Can we trust Him to come through when the going is rough?

Well, I am out on my limb; and I am not going to turn back, unless the Lord cuts off the limb and I fall. I felt that I had to look for His will in my life *now*. If I waited until I retired, I very well might be dead before I reached sixty-two.

All the plans Lawrence and I had made together were cancelled now. I realized that we have to seek first the kingdom of God. Then "these things shall be added." Both he and I had been preoccupied in earning a living, rearing a family, and taking care of our own needs.

Surely Lawrence would have been a more active church member and walked closer to God, if he had lived to retire. It is difficult to discipline oneself when you work rotating shifts with only one Sunday off a month. I couldn't help but wonder, if he had known that he was going to leave this world at such an early age, would he have had the same attitude toward Christian service? It seemed to me there was a lesson in his life and his death. If I didn't learn something from them, it would be a terrible waste of a precious opportunity.

Shortly after I quit working, my pastor sent me a leaflet that had come to his office. The Lily Foundation of Indianapolis, Indiana, was sponsoring a writers' conference at Lake Placid, Florida. This is about one hundred and thirty miles from our home. They were renting the Presbyterian conference grounds, inviting Christian writers to participate. The purpose of the conference was to teach Christian writers to write for the secular press. It was a long-range plan to upgrade today's literature. It was necessary to submit two pages of your writing; and if it was felt that your work had potential, you would be asked to come, tuition free.

I didn't know what to do. I'd have to drive—alone. I didn't know anyone else who was going or even interested in submitting his work.

I submitted my work because it seemed there was something providential about the conference coming at a time when I could drop everything and go. At any earlier time in my life responsibilities would have kept me from attending. On January 2 I received the invitation. How about that? A new year, a new experience, an opportunity for me to learn! God was letting things fall into shape for me after all!

All during the month of January I looked forward to the conference, both with apprehension and anticipation. I wanted to go—I was anxious to have my work evaluated and learn more about writing. But at the same time I was afraid to venture out. I didn't know how I would feel about taking that trip by myself or walking into a new experience without knowing one person there.

As I spent long hours preparing the work I was to submit, my mind raced ahead. Sometimes it sought small excuses to stay home. Sometimes it seemed that my brain would burst, just trying to imagine what it would be like when I got there.

6

Another Tragedy

ON SUNDAY EVENING, January 18, 1970, two days before the conference was to begin, I had a telephone call. It was so unexpected that I had no time to prepare for it. Picking up the phone, I recognized the voice of Martha Asche. Martha, president of our women of the church, often called me about various details—church nursery, youth plans, etc. Nothing in her tone of voice indicated that this call was any different.

"How are you, Martha?"

"Not good at all. Elliott Griffin just died, and I can't find my new list for the prayer chain. Will you find out whom I'm supposed to notify and call them for me?"

"Certainly I will, but what happened?"

"I don't have any information except that it was a plane crash. I don't even know if it was Eastern or a private plane. I have to hurry. Charles and I are going to his home."

In the next ten minutes I went through everything I had been through when Lawrence died. I cried harder than I had then because the shock triggered a flow of tears that I can usually control. I called the necessary people to inform them of the tragedy, but I could not bring myself to go to the Griffin home. It was dark; they lived a long way away; *and,* old chicken me, I simply did not want to go through this grief again. But I had to, it was impossible to put it out of my mind. I prayed most of the night. Even listening to the eleven o'clock news gave me no details about the tragedy. Elliott was an Eastern pilot. I finally decided that it must have been a big crash and they were holding the news pending notification of the families. It was one of the worst nights I ever spent.

When Lawrence died, we had a little warning. But I had seen Elliott in the narthex of the church that morning. Tall and handsome, he was only thirty-six years old. Their children were younger than any of mine. Elliott had a real passion for life. He was an elder in our church and active on all sorts of committees. His personality defied description. Everyone loved Elliott. He was one of Christ's most jubilant servants, but he was gone. How *could* he be dead? I saw him this morning, full of life!

The morning paper told me that he had died in a South Dade bean field in a small plane with three other people—two men and a young boy. The plane was demolished. The wreckage was so scattered that they couldn't even determine who the pilot was.

I spent a miserable day. Should I stay home from the writer's conference? The minister asked me not to. There were more than enough people to do what should be done for Betty and the children. It was an endless, restless sort of a day. Writing was impossible. I cleaned the car and packed for the trip, thinking about the two fathers who had left the earth at such a young age. And the eight young people—Betty's three and my five—what effect will these deaths have on them?

Betty requested that the church people not send flowers but instead contribute to a memorial fund in Elliott's name.

The people I talked to that day were dumbfounded by the sudden tragedy. Yet there persisted the idea that something especially good would come from it. The lives of four people had been snuffed out within minutes—no survivors, no one to tell what had happened, no one who knew what they were thinking in the last seconds of their life. All four were Christians. They left the world with a resounding jolt and plummeted into heaven without prior warning.

The Spirit of God moves mysteriously in your life and mine. What's up ahead? The most carefully laid plans can be torn asunder in one swift stroke!

7

Inspiration

TUESDAY MORNING I left early, out Tamiami Trail, up Route
27 to Lake Okeechobee, a lonely, desolate stretch of the Florida Everglades. I don't think that my husband would ever
have let me do that. He would have argued, "Suppose you
have a flat tire? Suppose the car breaks down? What will
you do then?"

I thought about these questions and decided that I would
leave them with the Lord. If it was His will that I attend
this conference, and it certainly appeared to me that it was,
then it was His business to get me there if I took proper pre-
cautions. If He saw fit not to do this, and I had car trouble—
Well I would have to think about it when the time came. The
old jalopy sped along the highway as if she knew where she
was going. I had no problems and arrived in plenty of time.

That day started one of the most invigorating inspirational
periods of my life. I have had little time to attend Christian
retreats. My husband always worked difficult shifts, and this
had kept me at home quite a bit. My five children were born
within seven years, and my responsibilities were clear, definite, and confining. Was it possible that the Lord had allowed
my life to be completely shattered so He could show me that
He was able to build another one, just as satisfying but
in another way?

The first evening, when everyone introduced themselves,
I was ready to slip out quietly and go home. It was impos-

sible to imagine what I was doing there with all these learned people. There were authors, lecturers, ministers, and doctors; and I was just me.

At the end of the introductions, Dr. Charles Shedd, who was conducting the conference, said, "I can just feel some of you squirming in your seat, wondering what you are doing here with all these successful people. Let me assure you that if you are here, you earned it. A literary consultant picked you forty people from one hundred and twenty manuscripts, as people who have something to write about and a talent to do it."

I felt a little better, but it still seemed to me that my ignorance must be glowing like a light in that group.

My roommate, Quin, was a reporter on the Titusville paper. She was a wonderful person. I learned that she was the first woman elder ever elected in her church, that her husband was an engineer with NASA at Cape Kennedy, and that she was keenly aware of social issues. Her cause was anyone who was not getting a fair shake.

Mostly, instead of telling me about herself, she helped me. We had classes from eight o'clock in the morning until nine o'clock at night. I had never worked so hard or had so much fun. After nine o'clock, Quin and I sat up for hours, discussing markets and writing in general. She read and criticized all the manuscripts that I had brought with me. She even gave me a new name. I had been writing under my legal name, Ruth B. Salls. She looked at the things that had been published and shook her head.

"That's too stiff and formal," she said. "You're not stiff and formal, and every Southern lady should have a double name."

So I became Betty Ruth. When I sold my first story under that name, she was as thrilled as I was.

The entire conference was based on the power of God to

help you if you let Him take hold of your life. God has all the ideas that you can use. All you have to do is set aside time to write and take the time to learn the craft of writing. Writing is a ministry that can change lives. The written word reaches people that the pulpit never touches!

We were told that if you want to write from your personal experience, make lemonade from your lemons. Take your saddest, most bitter experiences and make something agreeable and palatable. Don't dwell in your emotional valleys. Write about your mountaintops too.

8

Victory in Death

UPON MY ARRIVAL back in Miami, our annual January missionary conference was in full swing. Elliott Griffin had been chairman of the committee to set up the conference. Bonnie told me that, when she attended his funeral on Wednesday morning, the church was filled and overflowing. She had sat in a chair outside.

The conference was the fruit of his work, and the entire week was electrified by his accident. The services were well attended, as if the people were straining to learn from Elliott's final efforts in their behalf.

The sanctuary and the fellowship hall were attractively decorated with flowers. Without thinking I asked, "Where did all the flowers come from?"

"Dorothy Cleland fixed them all," I was told.

No further questions were needed. I knew that she had gone to Betty Griffin as she had come to me and suggested that some of the flowers be saved for the living. Dorothy Cleland had been at work again. Her whole life was centered on comforting, inspiring, and teaching the living to walk close to God. The physical evidence of her work was everywhere.

It was a beautiful and fitting tribute to Elliott. Although we could never look on his face again in this life, the mere presence of his funeral flowers in the church symbolized his living spirit and his walk with God.

No, the grave did not hold Elliott. The strength of his spirit was felt there at the mission conference, inspiring and comforting those saddened by his bodily departure.

The conference ended Sunday with the morning services dedicated to Elliott. The speaker was a personal friend of his, a missionary in Puerto Rico.

Mario E. Rivera is partially supported by our church, but not officially by our presbytery. A graduate of Columbia Seminary, he had been a minister in Columbus, Georgia. The Lord spoke to him in a convincing way one day and led him to open a small mission church in Puerto Rico. He went to the mission board, but they did not approve his plans; so he stepped out in faith and did what he believed was God's bidding. Elliott, in his flights to Puerto Rico, often called or visited Mr. Rivera and was enthusiastic about the work of the Holy Spirit in his ministry.

That Sunday morning Mr. Rivera brought a message that our congregation will not forget for many years. We were privileged to hear him first in the adult Sunday school class. Dorothy Cleland, who is our regular teacher, turned the whole hour over to him. The Holy Spirit filled the classroom as Mario spoke.

He spoke first of his ministry in Georgia. He had worked long hours, day after day, to add to the membership of his church and to serve the Lord.

In his own words he told us: "I visited the sick. I worked on my sermons. I attended the committee meetings. I counseled the depressed. I encouraged the willing. I prayed for the youth. And I saw no fruits of my labors.

"Realizing this, in agony I sat in my study one day and

asked God what was wrong. Where had I failed? What was I doing that wasn't right?"

And God brought conviction to his soul. Mario drew on the chalkboard an illustration of his answer from the Lord.

I did this.

I did that.

I worked hard.

I prayed to God.

His *I* was bigger than his God.

That day he died to self and let God take over his ministry. He asked God what to do next. Then he opened his Bible and read, "the church in thy house."*

He stared at it for a while and became convinced that God was sending him home to start a church in his house. He owned a rather ordinary home in Puerto Rico, which he had bought after the Korean War on the GI Bill; and this was the house in the message that God was sending him through the Spirit and the Word.

A few days later, this message was confirmed by the real estate agent who took care of his house. A special delivery letter came: "Your tenants have moved and your house is empty. What shall I do?"

He sent a telegram: "Leave it empty. I'm coming."

Without the sanction of the World Missions board, he went home to build *a church in his house*. He had nothing to go on except that God had spoken to him. In his church there were no pews, so he used empty paint cans, boxes, and suitcases. A door fell off the closet, so he put legs on it and made

---

*Philemon 1:2.

a table. Every Sunday he prepared for services, and no one came to his church.

His mother cried tears of disappointment. "Mario, you have made a mistake. No one wants to worship here."

But he calmly replied, "This is God's church. He will provide the membership."

His first convert was his fourteen-year-old niece. "Uncle," she said, "I want to be baptized and join your church. I want Christ in my heart."

And it was done. God's church had a membership of *one*. Four months later, the girl died of leukemia. Mario's only Christian convert lay in a casket.

Her parents were filled with bitterness. "Where is your God now?" they demanded. "Where was your God when my child was dying?"

"He's crying with you, just as He was when His Son was dying," he told them.

The church was renamed in her honor, the Barbara Ann Roessler Memorial Church. And the Holy Spirit began to add to its number. Barbara's parents and many of her family became Christians. The story of her death and her salvation spread throughout the city, and her ministry grew in death just as Mario's ministry grew in life. Her story, told through Mario's lips, brought many people to know Jesus Christ.

The church is strong now, with missions of its own. They are building a library to be named the Elliott Griffin Memorial Library, dedicated to bring God's Word to the masses in Puerto Rico. Yes, good can come from the death of a young person.

The power of the Holy Spirit penetrated that Sunday school room. Twenty-five adults walked out of the class much closer to God than they had been one hour earlier.

At the eleven o'clock service in the sanctuary, Mr. Rivera

spoke again. This time the service was dedicated to Elliott, in prayer that his death could bring good to the congregation and to the community.

The church was filled to capacity. Special flowers were placed on the altar in his memory, and there was an air of hushed expectancy. Saddened though we were by his death, and the loss of the three people who died with him, we expected God's presence in a way that would prove that all things do work together for good to those who love Him and are called according to His purpose.

9

My Time Is Running Out

FROM HIS POCKET Mario drew a letter, rumpled and tattered, and began to speak.

"There are no accidents. When death comes to a child of God, it is because God allowed it. He is in command. He has the power to change lives and He has the power to perform miracles. I have in my hand a miracle. I cannot explain why I have kept it. It is my custom to read a letter, either file it or make notations on my calendar, then throw the letter away. I never keep letters in my pocket. But this one I kept, though I did not know why I was doing it. It is a letter from Elliott Griffin. I did not know until I arrived here that I was bringing it home to his widow."

And then he read the letter:

Dear Rev. Rivera,

I hope you will excuse the informality of this letter, but since talking to you last in San Juan I have been busy arranging details for our upcoming world missions conference, and *my time is running out*. Therefore I want to send this invitation to you without further delay.

If your schedule permits, we would feel privileged to have you speak to our Adult Sunday School class at 9:40 A.M. and also to preach at the 11:00 A.M. service the 25th of January.

We hope this time and date will be satisfactory to you, but if not, please call the church when you arrive, and we will arrange a time that is convenient for you.

We are anxiously awaiting to hear more about the wonderful blessings God is working though you and your church in Puerto Rico.

Respectfully yours,
Elliott M. Griffin

Intense anguish is the only way to describe my feelings that morning as I listened to Mario preach. What could God be telling us by allowing these tragedies? How would God reveal His will to the people who heard Mario's stirring sermon? These were my thoughts as I listened.

"My time is running out."

The Spirit of God moves mysteriously in your life and mine. What's up ahead? The most carefully laid plans can be torn asunder in one swift stroke! There is no such thing as chance or accident. It was no accident that Elliott was in that plane. The Lord was working in his life and in the lives of his wife and children. Elliott had decided not to fly that day. But just as the plane started to take off, one of the men called to him, "Come on, Griff, just take a little ride."

Elliott was the most experienced pilot in the plane. He flew as a crop duster long before he went to work for Eastern. Most likely he had the skill to bring it out of the spin. But God put him in the back seat. Imagine if you will, what his thoughts were, knowing they were in trouble, knowing he was more skilled, yet unable to reach the controls. There are no accidents. *His time was running out.*

I do not believe that Elliott knew his time here on earth was running out. The letter, written seven days before he died, was a paradox. It meant what we all mean when we say we are busy. There isn't enough time in the day to do everything we want to do. We rush around engrossed in business, pleasure, and family; and all the time we're doing this, *our time is running out* here on earth. If we push God into the background of our lives, we may have to face Him and tell Him why before we have time to rectify our action. If you serve yourself before you serve the Lord, you may *never* get time on this earth to serve God. We can be called home at any moment, in a flash as He did Elliott, or in a year as He did Lawrence.

Neither of them realized that God's hand had marked him for death. *Their time was running out,* and there was no earthly indication that death was going to occur. Even though Lawrence's illness was recognized forty-five days before his final operation, he did not look like a sick man. No one was more surprised than his surgeons, for they had made thorough tests and were sure that he could withstand the operation. It never occurred to me that he would not recover from surgery. I've wished a thousand times that I had not allowed the operation. But then he would have died a horrible cancer death. Cancer was not the ultimate cause of Lawrence's death. The operation was apparently successful. After the operation, the Lord just called him home with a heart condition. This condition developed in spite of the fact that he was given cardiograms for several days prior to the operation to be sure that he could withstand the surgery.

There in the crowded church the air was charged with a sense of the Holy Spirit's presence and I became convinced that *my time is running out* too. Every hour of my life belongs to Christ. My need to utilize each day for His glory was uppermost in my mind. What would I do if I had only a few hours to live? I'm sure I would turn to God.

But why wait? Who can tell? Like Lawrence, there could be a tiny tumor in my body now that will take my life next year. Or like Elliott, an accident could put me in heaven before I arrived home from church. Or as in the book of Revelation, the end time could begin at any moment. Am I a sheep or a goat? Have I followed God or ignored His teachings? If today is my judgment, what will be the heavenly verdict?

The Spirit of God moves mysteriously in your life and mine. What's up ahead? The most carefully laid plans can be torn asunder in one swift stroke!

Faith is the door that opens to give you all the things that Christ has for you. If you have not faith, you have not the things that God has for you. Our friendship with God demands response. What have we done to cement this relationship today? Our Father has set the path; and He says, "This is the way, walk ye in it."*

*Isaiah 30:21.

10

Strength for Every Day

IT WAS FIVE MONTHS since Lawrence died and the week after Elliott's funeral. I looked back to see how far we had come and how much we had adjusted. There were many details that came to my mind.

Holidays were something that I never wanted to face again, but they are inevitable and it was necessary to find a way to cope with them. The first holiday after Lawrence's death was Labor Day, less than a week after his funeral.

The girls wanted to take a picnic lunch to the Keys. I felt I couldn't endure an outing of this kind. Barbara was just home from the hospital and too sick to be left by herself. I used this for an excuse not to go, although we could have asked someone to stay with her. It didn't seem like a holiday, and I wondered if I would ever enjoy celebrating anything again. I tried to persuade the girls to go without me, but they were really in no holiday mood either. They stayed home too, and we labored.

I was still working on the thank-you notes. Penny enlisted everyone else, and they redecorated my bedroom. It was thoughtful of them and I appreciated it. I'm sure they were thinking that if the drapes and the spread (everything easily changed) were new, the room would be more bearable for me.

It only made me realize that, hard as they tried, the emptiness inside me would not be filled by new surroundings. Lawrence was gone and I had to make a new life, but any attempt to forget him would be futile. Instead I had to learn to live without him. If you lost your right arm, I don't think you could forget *that*. Even when you learned to use your left hand for everything, you would still be quite aware that it was your *left* hand. It was the same way with losing Lawrence. I realized early that I could not forget him by changing my surroundings. I could clearly see that some pain was inevitable. Escape was impossible. I had to learn to live in my world and let the wound heal from the inside. To avoid familiar places now would mean that I could never feel comfortable there.

Everything that I did for the first time was painful. I even cried in the gas station the first time I filled the car after the funeral. The attendant was the same one who waited on us the day I took Lawrence to the hospital for his final operation.

The attendant was a friendly fellow, and it had looked backwards to him to see me driving and my husband sitting in the passenger seat.

He had quipped, "Hey, how do you rate a chauffeur today?"

Lawrence told him that he was on his way to the hospital for surgery and could not drive. Of course nothing was said to indicate the seriousness of his illness.

So when the attendant saw me again, in his ever cheerful manner he said, "How's your husband?"

It was perfectly understandable that he didn't know. After all, the only contact that we had with him was at the service station. Not every person reads the obituaries (Miami is a big place) and no one knows everything all the time.

Tears fell down my cheeks as I said, "He died."

Shock replaced the cheerfulness in his voice. It changed to sympathy and then impatience with himself for his blundering question.

The incident was to be repeated so often that I came to expect it and braced myself when I conducted business with someone Lawrence had known. Through the months I came to accept these situations and could discuss his illness and death without choking.

Our next major holiday was Thanksgiving. I was spared the traditional Thanksgiving feast because the girls wanted to go camping. They invited a mixed group to go with them, so that meant I had to go too.

The preparations were a little on the miserable side. We always attended the Thanksgiving Eve service at church. The girls weren't much interested in that. They were tired and had a long way to go to finish packing for the trip.

We were beginning to realize how much Lawrence's physical presence had meant to family fun. On other camping trips, Lawrence checked the gas lanterns and stove, bought the fuel, and made sure all the equipment was in order.

No such leadership on this trip! At the last minute Jeannie found that the poles to the tent had been left in the mountains. After Lawrence flew home and we came back in such a hurry, friends and relatives went to the cabin to close it and bring home what they thought we would need. The tent arrived all right, but the umbrella part necessary for putting it up was still in the mountains. So I bought another tent. It was our good fortune to find a used tent, bigger than the old one and easier to erect.

The camp stove was still in the mountains also, so we borrowed one. The gas lanterns didn't work, so we bought a kerosene lantern and left the others with a neighbor to fix.

Through a series of unusual incidents we arrived at the

campsite on Thanksgiving Day with no fuel for the gas stove. I rummaged in the camping trailer and found a small emergency burner the boys were able to make work. We made coffee on that and cooked the rest of the dinner on a charcoal fire. We ate a delicious meal under the trees with the next door neighbors, the family of Barbara's fiance. They brought the turkey, homemade pies, and lots of salad. We baked potatoes, made giblet gravy, and cooked the vegetables on the grill. It *did* work out, although nothing seemed to be the same as when Lawrence took care of things. We proved to ourselves that we could do it. There was no need to quit camping. We would just have to shuffle our responsibilities a little and streamline our equipment.

When Thanksgiving Day was over, the long weekend stretched ahead. This was camping as I had never known it. Of course the young people were interested in different things than I was. They took long hikes and long drives. When I was with them, I sometimes felt like a fifth wheel.

Youth walks through the woods relentlessly, moving constantly, sometimes exuberantly singing a silly song. Middle age walks slowly, taking in every flower, every tree and bush. Could I walk through the woods with these teenagers? Could I ever grow accustomed to their pace? Or should I stay a block or a half-mile behind by myself, remembering that a year ago Lawrence and I walked in these woods together, leisurely, never thinking that our lives would be interrupted in such a short time?

I couldn't endure either way without help; so my prayer became "Lord make me thankful. Make me thankful that we can still enjoy camping even though Lawrence isn't here. Make me thankful for this group of young people that I have to strain to keep up with. Without them in front, I'd be tempted to lag behind, to grow old too soon."

During the following days He did make me thankful. He filled my hours with His own companionship in place of Lawrence's. As I learned to walk with Him, He even gave me a few ideas for articles and sent me home refreshed and eager to sit at my typewriter. It was not the Thanksgiving I would have chosen, but it was satisfying—the first Thanksgiving Day of our new life.

Christmas was another story. It was hard for me to capture the Christmas spirit. Too often while shopping I found myself wandering through the men's wear or sporting goods department. All at once I would be shocked out of my listlessness by the realization that I had no need to do this. There was no one to buy a man's gift for.

Christmas with no new shirts under the tree, no new guns or power tools to ponder over! It was worse, far worse than the first year Jeannie announced that she wanted no more toys for Christmas. When all the girls outgrew toys, Christmas changed at our house: instead they clamored for hair driers, watches, jewelry, and cosmetics. Now, this new turn of events had substituted nothing. It brought only emptiness. No new shirts, no sports equipment, no new tools. I wasn't ready for a Christmas like that, but it came.

In God's own time it came just as everything does. I can't say that I had an exciting, wonderful time. It was different, the first Christmas without a man in the house.

The cards came from faraway places addressed to Mr. and Mrs. Lawrence Salls and had to be answered with a personal note. Could it be there were still people who didn't know of his death? Lawrence died in August; Lawrence died in August. I wrote until the words were branded on my heart, and I was forced to take refuge in the comfort of the future resurrection as I never had before. It was only through the death and resurrection of Christ that I was able to accept the death of my husband. The knowledge that in Christ we shall meet again and celebrate an eternity of Christmas days made this one bearable.

The girls went out of their way to buy me nice gifts so that I wouldn't miss the ones their dad usually gave me. I was amazed by the amount of money and time they spent to make Christmas happy. Nevertheless, the day had its dragging hours. It was one of our hardest times, but each succeeding Christmas would be a little easier.

Lawrence *is* with Christ. This is the important thing. Our problem is to adjust ourselves to his physical absence. This has been easier because I have received help from the sense of his spiritual presence.

The Comforter who had helped me in the beginning was still on the job. The verse that came to me when Lawrence died, "I will not leave you comfortless" sprang from *Living Gospels* as, "No, I will not abandon you or leave you orphans in the storm—I will come to you!"* This meant to me that He is here, ready to lead us as we accept His help. The healing touch of the Master Physician was at work.

*John 14:18.

11

Life Goes On Relentlessly

CHRISTMAS OVER, we turned our efforts toward the next big event, Barbara's wedding. She had become engaged before Lawrence's illness. Her dress, long billowy clouds of lace, had been purchased almost a year ago. Her illness and Lawrence's death postponed the big day, but now it was time to get everything accomplished.

We trimmed down the size of the wedding party as much as possible. There would be no flower girl and no ringbearer. A big splash did not seem appropriate so soon after her father's death; however, when you have four sisters, weddings have a way of becoming large, no matter how much you trim.

We made the bridesmaids' gowns in rainbow colors with large picture hats to match. We held lengthy conferences with the florist, the baker, and the photographer. Life took on a furor that is unparalleled at any other time. The order of each day was sewing, fittings, invitations, plans, and details, details, details.

Through it all ran a thread of uneasiness. I had never attempted anything this big before without Lawrence's help. I didn't know if I could do it or not; but we waded through, day after day. Takeout food from the Burger Castle became our mainstay. Finally the week before the wedding arrived, and it was as if we were living in a wind tunnel. The day was bearing down on us relentlessly, and it would come whether we were ready or not.

Penny arrived at the airport eight days before the wedding. Without her I don't believe that I could have handled all the last minute happenings. She flitted from one project to another, arranging bows and artificial baby's breath on the bride's knife, sewing emergency stitches, helping with the bridal tea and the rehearsal dinner. I was deeply grateful that God had spared my husband's life until the girls were mature. It seemed to me that they all began to grow up the day we learned their dad had cancer. It was obvious that I could count on them when I needed help. My mind went back to the days when they were children. I knew that, though Lawrence was gone, God had blessed me richly when He allowed us to bring up our children together.

The frenzied days of preparation finally reached a climax. The big day was at hand. Anything that hadn't been done by now would just have to go undone. We had lists and more lists, the "don't forgets."

When Penny awoke that morning, she said, "I hate to remind you of this, but remember Daddy kept telling Barbara he wasn't going to walk down the aisle and give her away? Well, he really isn't."

Momentarily, it was something to think about. From the time Barbara had become engaged, he had maintained that he was too shy to walk down the aisle in front of all those people. It made you wonder, was it simply teasing or did he have a vague premonition that he wouldn't be here when the time came?

No time to ponder on that. My mind was spinning and I spent the day in a daze. A hurried trip to an open-air flower stand for the mums to make the bridesmaids' baskets, a stop at the doughnut shop for goodies for breakfast—these were all things that I could have left to Lawrence if he had lived. Why must *everything* take so much time?

The girls and I converged en masse on the beauty parlor. It was a chance to relax as the shampoo girl oozed the rich, thick suds through my hair.

I instructed the stylist, "Yes, a wedding! It's important that it turn out well. A bubble, and candlestick it in the back, please."

Thirty minutes under the drier—time to think about tying all the loose ends! The odd jobs that Lawrence would have done had been handed out one by one to the neighborhood teens. I prayed that everything would be done on time, that the details would remain details, and that this would be a solemn, holy occasion.

The comb-out, and all was well. My hairdo was short, smart, and simple. The girls were having theirs elaborate and stylish. No need to wait for them, I called someone to pick me up.

The homestretch! If nothing serious happens in the next few hours, we've made it. A check on the church revealed that no one had turned on the air conditioner. It took several calls to find someone who understood the mysterious workings of that machine. The cake had been delivered; the tables were set up. The church was decorated. All the corsages and boutonnieres had arrived—no slipups there. Matches and tapers in place to light the candles, guest book on the stand by the door—everything was in order. Nothing left to do but dress for the big moment.

By this time I was running on Someone else's energy. I never thought that I could do it by myself, and suddenly I realized that I wasn't by myself. The Holy Spirit had provided a way for each detail to fall into place. Even though

Lawrence was gone, dozens of *people* had helped me get to this point.

My brother-in-law Bob, handsome in his white jacket, took over the last few minutes. A good friend was in the vestibule to direct the procession. My next-door neighbor stood ready and waiting with a movie camera. The photographer finished the prewedding pictures, and I gingerly walked down the aisle on the arm of the groom's younger brother. Excitement of the occasion gave the ushers unaccustomed dignity and poise. Everything progressed right on schedule. In the candle-lit church the guests sat hushed and waiting.

One by one my four daughters marched slowly down the aisle, each in a different pastel color. Then, "Here Comes The Bride," and Barbara entered on the arm of her uncle. Someone behind me stifled a gasp. Stark realization had struck a friend. On the biggest day of her life, Barbara had no father to give her away.

By now my thoughts were different. This was the child that was doomed to die at birth. Twenty-one years ago, my obstetrician sat on the edge of my hospital bed and told me that surgery was imminent. There was almost no hope that they could save her life, but they would make a last-ditch effort. God intervened! Even as the surgeon had prepared for the operation, another way was provided. Now she was on her way down the aisle, radiant and well as she began her married life. Without her father, yes, but living proof that His love reigns! When there is no hope, He creates it. When help and comfort are needed, He supplies it.

I can't say that I remember much about the ceremony itself. Mostly I prayed that Barbara wouldn't faint. An ammonia capsule was in the pocket of every man in the wedding party, just in case; but there was no need for them. God had promised, "They that wait upon the LORD shall renew their strength; they shall mount up with wings as eagles; they shall run, and not be weary; and they shall walk, and not faint."*

The doctor had told Barbara that in times of much stress or excitement, she still might faint. The Lord took care of everything. It was beautiful and solemn and Christian—as a wedding should be—and a tribute to her father, even in his absence. He had provided for us a Christian background that was needed for the foundation of such a wedding. He gave us the material and emotional assets to carry on after his death. Even his absence could not mar the happiness of this occasion.

The Spirit of God moves mysteriously in your life and mine. What's up ahead? A brand new family was formed that night. The mysteries of their life together were just beginning to unfold.

*Isaiah 40:31.

12

It's Not Always Lemonade

BEFORE THE WEDDING I thought that the worst thing in the world would be to go through the ceremony without Lawrence. I dreaded it. However, the excitement took me through the evening without any problem. The worst was yet to come.

I was as stiff and sore all day Sunday as if I had been horseback riding. We had studied intently at least six wedding books, but none of them prepared me for the mountain of mess to be cleaned up after the festivities. More than half of our living room floor was covered with gifts still in their elegant wrappings. The table of gifts Barbara displayed before the wedding took up one whole side of the room. The leftovers from the reception, the decorations, and all the girls' dresses combined to make our living room, kitchen, and family room look like a disaster area. I had no idea what to do with all the stuff.

After the wedding someone had said, "Nuts, let's go to bed and leave it like it is. We can clean it up in the morning." It didn't take any persuasion for me to do just that. I beat everyone to the hall door that leads to the bedrooms!

What I would have done without the girls and the groom's brothers I will never know. They worked most of the following day cleaning up the aftermath.

By Monday morning the house was somewhat livable.

Penny had two and one-half days left for shopping, and we spent two hectic days visiting all the new shops that had opened since her last visit.

Wednesday I took her to the airport. She forgot her coat and we knew she was heading into a snowstorm. I crept home in the five o'clock traffic. By this time my brain was completely pickled. I wasn't thinking at all. We could have opened her suitcase, taken out a heavy sweater for the trip, and called her husband to bring another coat to the airport, But I went home for the forgotten coat instead. Returning to the airport, I was now on the other side of the four-lane highway and free of rush-hour traffic. My speedometer registered between 70 and 90 miles an hour all the way. The only parking place was a long way from the terminal. I ran through the parking lot, across the lobby, and down the long concourse. I made it just as the pilot was entering the plane. Penny was already on board and he took the coat to her. I was completely drained. Linda's fiance drove the car home.

The next day I was exhausted. Life was closing in on me. There was all kinds of activity at home. Jeannie was painting her bedroom and needed help, but I couldn't do it.

Linda was buying a new car; and I, who had never before financed anything, found myself checking interest rates and making decisions that were completely new to me.

About this time I realized I had lost a check for $700.00. I felt as if I were drowning. Instead of water, I was engulfed in money problems, taut nerves, and exhaustion.

All day Friday I fought to keep out of bed. I was in physical pain and mental anguish. Even in the first days after Lawrence died, I had not allowed myself to sink to such a severe state of depression.

I went to the photographer to pick up Barbara's proofs. Then I went with Linda to buy her car. It was Good Friday.

night. I always had gone to communion on this night and never should have let myself do anything else. The monster that was growing inside me was consuming me. It had been weeks since I enjoyed a free moment. There was always something that had to be done. Instead of going to the communion service as I planned, I let myself be carried along with the tide. Good Friday night was spent untangling problems at the car dealer. Silently, I fumed.

Saturday morning I had a violently upset stomach and a headache. I could not get out of bed. The girls were changing bedrooms and I hardly heard them. They really worked. At noontime they were tired, so they quit working and went to the beach. I got up a little later and saw that they had rushed off in such a hurry that the lunch dishes were still on the table. This always depresses me. The whole house can be in disorder and wouldn't bother me too much, but I *hate* dirty dishes on the table. I cleaned them up and ran the dishwasher. Then I took a bath, dressed, and waited for the girls to come home.

I had flowers to take to Lawrence's grave, and I wanted to get a small ham and some goodies for Easter, the next day. At 6:10 Barbara came from next door and told me that Linda's new car had broken down. She and Vern were going to get them and tow the car home. Twilight was approaching. I knew that if I was going to get the flowers on the grave, I would have to drive over there myself. I was light-headed and dizzy. But there wasn't much traffic between the house and the cemetery, so I went. Before I arrived someone had put flowers in the vase at the headstone, so I had no place to put mine. I looked in the car trunk for a container but found none. That was a wasted trip. By the time I returned home, it was dark and I didn't have the strength to go back to the cemetery or to the store to shop for Easter.

Linda and Jeannie came home, both disgusted about the car. They changed their clothes and went right out again to a barbeque. We still hadn't cleaned house or planned an Easter dinner. Bonnie was sick all this time, so she could be of no help.

I wanted to go to the Easter sunrise service, but the girls were worn out and I felt too sick to drive. I had looked forward to going because everyone was expecting an exceptionally good service. Senator Hatfield of Oregon was to be the speaker and Anita Bryant the soloist.

My dejection and my rejection of myself increased during the Sunday school hour when the members of the class described the sunrise service in glowing terms. The teacher really hit a sore spot when she ended the class by saying, "I hope you have the best Easter ever. The test of this will be how close you are to Christ."

That did it! My Easter was miserable. My fellowship with Christ was broken. I could hardly stand to think that I had allowed myself to put Linda's car before Good Friday communion. I felt no relationship to God at all.

In church the sermon did me little or no good. For the first time since I could remember, the front of the church had not been made beautiful for Easter. One small arrangement was on the communion table, little more than a table centerpiece. I was thoroughly disgusted with myself for not ordering lilies for the church in memory of Lawrence, instead of buying those insensible plastic flowers for his grave—and not even getting them on the grave!

I dropped off a friend after church, so the girls were home ahead of me. When I got home, Jeannie already had gone to look for a birthday cake that Barbara and Vern forgot to get the day before. Bonnie was still sick, and Linda was watering flowers in the yard.

The kitchen had been upset since yesterday. No lunch had been started. The towels and an old sandy sheet from yesterday at the beach had been thrown on one of the living room chairs. All I could think of was that it looked as if we had given up living in a decent manner.

I tried to talk calmly to Linda about putting God first, especially at Easter. I suggested that the freak thing that had happened to her car (a screw came loose, fell into the motor, and tore it to pieces) could be a result of pride and vanity and preoccupation with herself. Then I said a few things about her flippant and disinterested attitude toward worship and God. I botched that up good and made her cry.

When Jeannie finally came home after lunch was over, I told her I resented the fact that it was already one o'clock on Easter Sunday and we still hadn't done one thing to get ready for Easter. I told her to let Barb and Vern find their own birthday cake if they forgot to buy one, and I made her very angry.

Then I began to cry. I've never been with anyone who had a nervous breakdown, but I think I was close to it. I could not control my emotions at all. The thing that really scared me was that my separation from God seemed complete.

The next day Jeannie was too exhausted and upset to go to school, so she slept until almost noon. By this time I thought I could talk to her calmly. That conversation didn't turn out well at all. She concluded that I was blaming her for her father's death and promptly packed her clothes in a large plastic garbage bag and ran away.

By this time I was taking tranquilizers, and they were doing no good. Jeannie came back before dinner and things began to calm down somewhat. After dinner I could feel myself getting numb from my teeth down to my toes. Only one other time had this ever happened to me—after my mother's funeral four years ago. My doctor had come and given me a shot. I slept twenty-four hours and woke up feeling fine.

I didn't want to upset the girls further, so I dialed the doctor from my bedroom phone. He was not on call. The answering service told me she had to know what was wrong or the doctor taking the calls would not answer.

I told her my husband had died recently and I had been having a bad week, that I already had taken my quota of tranquilizers with no results and desperately needed help. The doctor didn't even give me the courtesy of a reply. The answering service called me back and told me to stop taking all medication until nine o'clock the next morning when I could talk to my doctor.

I was furious. I threatened to call my own doctor at his home and tell him that I had been refused medication. She relayed the information to the doctor on call. He called me back and we fought. He intimated that I was addicted to drugs and that, if I had any sense at all, I could handle my emotional problems without medication. I had visions of being in the psychiatric ward of the county hospital before morning.

Even though I told him I had been given a shot under similar circumstances four years before, he refused. By now I was in a much worse state than when I first placed the call. I dialed my doctor's home number a few times, but the line was busy.

Next I called the surgeon who attended my husband when he died and explained that I was having a bad time. I had taken three tranquilizers and they had done me no good. While he was deciding what would help the most, I told him I would be all right if he could give me something more powerful to enable me to sleep. He did this gladly, and I sent the girls to the drugstore to pick up the prescription. I shudder to think of what would have happened to me that evening if I had not been put to sleep.

At 2:30 A.M. I awoke and fought with myself in the dark for a long time. I had not asked the doctor if I could take another pill if I didn't sleep through the night, and I was afraid of an overdose. I got up and went to the kitchen for a cup of tea. First I read, then I cried. About four o'clock I went back to bed.

A few weeks before the wedding Barbara had come running into my bedroom about midnight to say that someone was trying to get in the back door. I called the police. They came right away but found no one. After they left, I loaded a shotgun and a pistol and took them into the bedroom with me. I had not given them another thought, and they were still there in the corner of the closet.

I don't know if I was dreaming or if I was awake, but every time I closed my eyes I could see the shotgun.

Then the thought popped into my mind, "Why don't you blow your brains out?"

I shook my head and rose up enough from my stupor to know that was a horrible idea. I dozed again and the same thing happened. This was repeated three or four times. I did not want to go to sleep, for fear I would walk in my sleep and actually shoot myself. I was afraid to unload the gun, indeed afraid to touch it in my state of mind. I had no desire for self-destruction; but every time I closed my eyes, this thought came involuntarily. It is the first and only time that I have felt the power of Satan. There was a presence in the room urging me to do something that I had no desire to do.

Even the words were not my own. "To blow your brains out" is not in my vocabulary. If this idea had originated with me, I would have said, "Why don't I shoot myself?"

I was in such bad mental and emotional condition that I

was not walking through the valley of the shadow of death; I was crawling through the gulley at the bottom of the valley!

But God had the answer. When Penny was a teenager, she rummaged through the things in my bedroom so often that Lawrence became angry one day and installed a lock on the bedroom door. Now this lock could be of help. I knew that if I could get out of the bedroom and lock the door, I would be safe. The gun would be inside the bedroom, and I had no idea where the key was. By this time it must have been about five o'clock. With a great deal of effort (because I was still drugged by the medicine and by intense depression), I took a blanket, locked the door, and went to sleep on the couch. I fell into an untroubled sleep immediately.

I awoke about seven, feeling better but shaken from my experience in the middle of the night. Still furious with the doctor who had refused to give me a sedative, I called my doctor at nine o'clock. My anger at his associate was in high key. The doctor was appalled at my experience, and his first order was to unload the shotgun right away. I'd never had any nervous disorder nor entertained thoughts of self-destruction, and he was aware of this. But I was crying so hard on the phone that he told me to come to his office for a prescription for antidepressant pills.

This was normally my time to write, but I was too upset to do that. I did a little housework, and cried. I read, and cried. I thought about myself as a potential suicide, and cried.

Then the mailman came with word that I had sold an article for a nice price to a national magazine. I didn't cry anymore. I had especially wanted to sell this article. It was a hobby article about Lawrence. It was just what I needed to pull me out of my doldrums. If anyone ever doubted the Lord's power, they should have seen me that day. I was so

happy that I did everything but turn handsprings. I knew I
didn't need the antidepressant or the good, fatherly talk I
had coming when I reached the doctor's office, but I kept
the appointment.

He was amazed at the change in me. I told him I already
had my pill and didn't need his.

He said, "Well, I have to admit the pills I was going to give
you would have taken about seven days to be effective. Yours
worked much faster. I have read that something can happen
to bring one out of deep depression immediately, but this is
the first time I have seen it happen."

The truth was that the Holy Spirit was at work in my life
again, and His power was greater than Satan's. There is no
doubt in my mind that God provided a way to cure my depression even before I turned to Him in need. Some people
might feel that it was a coincidence—my selling a story on
that particular day. I feel that it was more than that. It was
God's care and His comfort and evidence of His strength. It
was all things working together for good to those who love
God and are called according to His purpose.

Reading my Bible that day, I found the following verse:
"God is faithful, who will not allow you to be tempted beyond
what you are able; but with the temptation will provide the
way of escape also, that you may be able to endure it."*

It was real to me that day! I was actually experiencing the
power of God as opposed to the power of Satan. The struggle
and the victory were real!

*1 Corinthians 10:13, NASB.

13

Climbing Out

MY ENCOUNTER with the power of the devil was a tremendous emotional experience. I was not to escape so lightly that there would be no aftereffects. Complete exhaustion overcame me; I felt absolutely drained. When my initial enthusiasm over selling the article had subsided, an empty, letdown feeling took its place. It was much like recuperating from an illness. You know it's over, yet you don't have the same feeling of health that you enjoyed before the illness struck. However, life goes on; and it is necessary to take care of everyday problems and solve them during your recuperation.

I was at church the next day on an errand, and the minister called to me from his study. Although it had not been my intention to do so, I found myself telling him about my harrowing week. I had been in far worse condition emotionally than I was the week that Lawrence died, and I was still pretty despondent over having allowed myself to acquire such a state of nerves.

He suggested that I was blaming myself too much. I had wanted to do what was right, and perhaps I had not made all the right choices; but that did not signal the end of the world. God *does* forgive, so there is no reason to walk around with a burden of self-incrimination.

This helped to straighten out my thinking somewhat. I was terribly ashamed of having let things get so out of hand. The worst part of the whole experience was a separation from God, a feeling that I had failed Him and could not reach out and fellowship with Him because of my part in such a miserable week. To be able to talk it out and to pray in the pastor's study helped me to set my feet on the right path again. I was not about to tell my family that I was in danger of shooting myself in the middle of the night, and the act of telling someone besides the doctor was a relief. To have a man who understood the Scriptures discuss it brought the incident into a perspective that I could handle. Before talking to him, it had loomed as something large and dark and dreadful in my background, something that I might never fully recover from. But as he prayed for my guidance, it was as if a large weight was lifted and a cloud that obscured my vision disappeared. I felt more like my old self again.

The following week almost everything that could have gone wrong did so. Linda was stopped by the police on the way home from work. The inspection sticker on the English Ford had expired. They didn't give her a ticket, but to continue driving it was inviting trouble. I really hate doing anything to a car. I'm a mechanical idiot. But I told her to drive my car, and I would have hers inspected.

We were certain that it would not pass inspection because the headlights worked only on the lower beam. But I could let it fail, and then it would be legal to drive it for ten days while we found someone who could fix it.

On the way I saw a four-car smashup and was shaking inside when I drove into the inspection station. The attendant was in a bad mood. A few months before I had my own car inspected, and he had been as friendly and helpful as could be. This was not his day! I aimed the car at the center of the runway. With a scowl he directed me to the far left. When he saw that my sticker had expired, he took it as a personal insult.

"You'll have to pay an extra dollar," he grumbled.

I had the money only in quarters, and he glared while I wasted his time counting out four dollars. The more surly he acted the more upset I became.

Then he said, "Try your windshield wipers."

I probably had not turned them on for five years, and it took me awhile to find the button.

He brought the machine that checks headlights and lined it up in front of the car. "Turn on your lights," he growled. I did.

"Now your upper beams," he snapped.

I knew they weren't going to work, and in my confused state of mind I didn't even know how to try them. Unaccustomed to a car with a standard shift, I had both feet busy—one on the brake and one on the clutch. It didn't occur to me to put the car in neutral. Not wanting to antagonize him further by hesitating, I quickly turned off the key and took both feet off the pedals. Too quickly! I took them off before the engine had died. The car lurched forward, and the attendant had to grab the machine and jump out of the way.

"Please excuse me," I said. "I just never drive this car."

By this time, I'm sure he was convinced that I had stolen it. "Whose is it?" he demanded.

"My husband's," I replied meekly, thinking that if I didn't get him calmed down he might have me arrested for reckless driving.

"Why isn't he here if you can't drive any better than this?" he roared.

"He died and we've kept the car so my children can get back and forth to work."

His face fell. He was a changed man! He became so embarrassed that he didn't bother to finish checking the lights. Calmly he told me what to do to check the brakes and came around the car to apply the sticker. It was over. I'd passed, and I just sat there looking miserable.

"It's OK. Take it easy," he said kindly.

I left in a hurry, before he realized that he hadn't finished checking the lights. We were all set with that car for another year. I resolved to have the headlights fixed as soon as possible.

When the girls got home that evening, they were dumbfounded to see the valid sticker, because they *knew* it could not pass.

Bonnie said, "Don't ever complain about how grumpy he was. If he had been in a good mood, you never would have passed. You must know that God was sitting in the seat beside you to get *that* car through!"

That was another milestone, one more thing accomplished; but I could not completely throw off the dejection I felt. I was exhausted, tired even when I woke up in the morning. And vitamins did no good.

Saturday I had another bit of good news. *Guideposts* was planning its twenty-fifth anniversary celebration with a two-day conference for writers. I had always wanted to meet Norman Vincent Peale and Catherine Marshall. There they were, both in one event. I was invited to come to New York for two days and attend the conference. The Lord was working overtime to heal my upset nerves! I sent in my reservation that same day, and it helped to know I had this to look forward to.

Sunday morning I got up as tired as if I had worked all night. Probably I had. There was no way I could settle down to sleep and rest. My troubles went to bed with me; and all night I hashed them over, even in my dreams.

At last I did the final thing that helped me throw off this troubled mood. I talked to Flo Hadley a few minutes at Sunday school about my experience with the gun in the middle of the night and asked her to come to lunch with me Wednesday. I was over the incident, and yet not over it. Wednesday she came to lunch, and we talked for several hours about God and the devil—the forces of evil against the forces of good.

She said, "You know, Betty, I have no doubt that it *was* the devil in your bedroom the other night. He has power, great power to use in this world. If you are doing anything worthwhile for God, Satan will hound you. He will stay on your trail. You see, the Lord has called you to write. The devil realized that you have something to say that will help people to find Christ. If he can get to you first, if he can snuff out your life or discourage you, then you will never follow Christ and be active in His ministry."

We talked about it from every angle. Flo explained Luke 22:31-32 to me: "Simon, Simon, Satan has asked to have you, to sift you like wheat, but I have pleaded in prayer for you that your faith should not completely fail."*

"In other words," she said, "Satan desires to capture you. Christ is praying for you. And that was the reason you were able to resist Satan's temptation. Christ was praying for you. I'm sure it was possible that you could have shot yourself; there was actually a battle between the forces of evil and the forces of good in your room that night."

This was exactly the feeling that I had experienced—a life and death struggle. If I hadn't fled from the room, I could have lost the battle.

It gave me a whole new concept of suicide, or any sin. Never before had I felt *driven* to do something against my

Living Letters.

own will. Having lived a sheltered, comparatively uneventful life, I had never really suffered. Death and tragedy had rarely touched me. My family lived in Dade County for fifty-four years, and my parents have over thirty descendants here; however, there are only three relatives in the cemetery—my parents and my husband. We'd never had a serious accident or a stillborn baby in this big family. Our finances had always been reasonably secure. I had never understood how a man or a woman, living an ordinary middle-class life, could possibly commit suicide or a crime against mankind. Now I have a new understanding. Given any toehold in your life, Satan enters, urges, tempts, entices you to do things that you normally wouldn't consider.

In a sermon that I heard recently, the minister declared, "For a child of God, the battle with Satan is a constant thing. If Satan is not bothering you, it's because he has captured your influence already and is satisfied with your life and your witness."

Before Flo left, she prayed, asking God to bring into my life people whom I could write about, and thanking Him for the influence that I could be for Christ. For the first time in two weeks, since I took that wild ride to the airport, I felt relaxed. For the first time I didn't ache in every bone. I spent the afternoon feeling very well.

Finally I was out of that valley of depression and on level, firm ground again! It felt great!

14

Not Again, God!

GOD HAD TO HAVE ME over my depression by Wednesday because only He knew what was to happen later in the day. The news came to me at 8:45 that evening. I had about six hours of peace. The torment that I suffered for two weeks finally subsided and I rested. It was a good thing, because my strength was needed.

Bonnie came home from prayer meeting and said, "You know what happened? Mr. Covington just died of a heart attack."

Mr. Covington was not a man that I knew well. His wife, Shirley, had worked in our Sunday school for several years. Up until a few months ago she had been junior department head and I had been primary department head.

My first thought was, *Oh no, God, not again! Not three young men in our church in just eight months!*

And yet I knew that you cannot question God. God's will *is.* There is no way to change it. The only balance that I could think of for this terrible thing was that God's comfort *is also.* I knew I had to do something to help Shirley. We never had been close friends, and I didn't know exactly where her house was. Already clothed in my pajamas, I reasoned that if the church knew about it, someone who knew her well would go to her. My decision was to stay home for that night.

I wasn't the least bit sure that I could go to her anyway. Instead I wrote her a letter, offering condolence and help from a veteran in grief.

Thursday morning was spent writing, but my thoughts kept gliding toward the Covingtons. A mutual friend called from her office to see if I knew how Shirley was feeling. It caused a twinge of guilt to tell her that I didn't know. Her call give me the nudge that I needed. When I phoned the church office to see what could be done, the preacher didn't send me, but his desire for me to go was loud and clear.

There was still an uneasy feeling about entering a bereaved home to face the same situation that I was experiencing. In addition to having all the problems of living without a husband, Shirley was pregnant. I wasn't acquainted with her well enough to know if she would be holding up or be absolutely crushed by the blow.

I dressed and went out to a hamburger stand for lunch, hoping to meet someone who had seen the family and could tell me what to expect. I did meet a friend, but she reminded me that this was Circle Thursday and the active women of the church had been in meetings all morning. I knew there was another large segment of women who were working and could not go until evening. That left only me, and I certainly was indebted to do my part after all the help I had received when Lawrence died. Visions of Shirley sitting at home all by herself sent me flying into action.

The visit with the family was one of the biggest blessings God could have planned for me. Shirley was a rock. Her mother-in-law was in agony, but Shirley comforted her and made plans for her well-being. The children were coming along reasonably well. Over it all, their Christian faith shone like a light. The mother-in-law went home with friends, and Shirley and I settled down to practical things. We discussed

Social Security and veteran's benefits that would keep them going financially.

I drove her to a shopping center to buy clothes for the two boys. They had nothing to wear that she felt was suitable for the funeral. By the time they were outfitted, she was very tired; but she wanted a black dress, and there were none in the maternity section of the department store. I was anxious to get her home. She was heavily sedated, pregnant, and looked as if she would fall on the floor any minute. She also had a history of premature babies, two of whom didn't live.

"If you will go home and rest, I'll make you a black dress. I can do it quicker than we can shop for one," I told her.

She was so tired she agreed. I left her with instructions to rest and told the children to tell people who called that she was too tired to talk.

I went to pick up Jeannie at school and fix dinner. Then I took the pattern books to Shirley, and she picked her pattern. After discussing the kind of material she wanted, I left in search of something suitable.

I sent up "quickie" prayers all the way to the store because I wanted to go to the Night Circle meeting. Unless the material appeared in a hurry I couldn't make it. The Lord was right beside me. I stopped at one store and there was my material. (I usually take hours to find what I want!) This was a remnant. The pattern, zipper, thread, and material cost only $3.20. The whole transaction took ten minutes. This was a direct answer to prayer. It happened so quickly that I was the first one to arrive at the Circle meeting.

What a meeting it was! Flo Hadley had the lesson, and it was so relevant that I could hardly believe my ears.

"A Ministry in Trouble" was the subject with which she

challenged us. Every one of us who has been through tribulation has the power to minister to another now having the same trouble. To think that she had been preparing this lesson for several weeks! It spoke directly to me. It told me that I was needed to help Shirley through her grief; and if my help was not forthcoming, I should be ashamed to call myself a Christian. A ministry to the troubled is the business of every Christian—a down-to-earth, one-to-one ministry that changes lives, a ministry that blesses both the one who receives and the one who gives.

"We need real action, straight from the Holy Spirit," she told us.

Through it all, I kept thinking about Flo's own ministry. She was neither my pastor nor my Sunday school teacher but a friend to whom I turned when I had a desperate need. Had she ignored me and been too busy to talk to me yesterday, I would have been too helpless to do anything for Shirley today. It was a wonderful evening of sharing. Our spirits were refueled as we planned the ways we could comfort the newly bereaved family, and we prayed for the blessing of the Holy Spirit to touch each of our lives.

The whole meeting pointed vividly to the fact that the minister of a church cannot possibly do all of the counseling, comforting, and praying for those in trouble in the community. Unless the members are active—each one in a ministry of his own motivated by the Holy Spirit—you have a dead church.

As soon as the meeting was over, I hurried home to cut out the dress. I planned to get up at daybreak and start to sew, hoping to have it done before four o'clock. God had a different plan. When I got in bed, I couldn't sleep. It wasn't a fussing, fretting lack of sleep like I had had during my two weeks of depression. I simply wasn't tired. Why waste time in bed if you aren't tired? Between midnight and one o'clock I sewed the dress together and completed everything but the armholes, the neckline, and the hem. There was nothing else to do until Shirley tried it on. After that, sleep came immediately.

The amazing thing was that the sewing was done correctly. I have poor eyesight and had never been able to sew on dark material at night, but this turned out exactly right. Someone had been at my elbow directing my work, or I surely would have sewed the right side to the wrong side and not known the difference until daylight.

In the morning I took the dress to Shirley to be fitted. Her brother and mother had arrived from North Carolina, and I was impressed with her family. Their Christian faith in the face of grief was an inspiration.

Mrs. Sellers, Shirley's mother, told me that history was repeating itself. At the age of thirty-eight, she had been widowed. Her youngest child was born just a few days less than nine months later. She didn't even know that she was pregnant when her husband died. She raised four children by herself.

Now Shirley at thirty-eight was a widow with three children, and pregnant. No family should have to bear such a burden twice, and in consecutive generations!

But, neither bitterness nor questioning was evident. The situation was accepted, and they were all busy trying to fit together the pieces of the old life to make a new one for Shirley and the family.

Financially the outlook wasn't good, but they were not destitute. In the darkness there came many blessings. They had no cemetery plot, so a friend gave Shirley one of his. Bob had no life insurance, but an anonymous person paid the funeral expenses in full. When she told me about these gifts, I thought of Christ and His borrowed tomb.

The healing power of the Holy Spirit through the presence and concern of Christian friends was evident. As when Lawrence and Elliott died, there was more food, more offers of help, more flowers, more of everything than the family thought possible. Money appeared in envelopes in the mail to tide them over until the Social Security and veteran's pension could be arranged. Everything—food, cards, flowers, gifts of money, and expressions of sympathy—was healing the crevices of pain and grief.

In the Christian an experience with deep sorrow creates a dedicated desire to help others in trouble once one's own grief has settled a little bit. Shirley mentioned this. She didn't hear Flo's lesson at the Circle meeting; but the night after the funeral, she was busy making plans to renew her own service to mankind. She had done nothing at Lawrence's death, nothing at Elliott's death; and yet here was all the help in the world when she needed it. It humbled her just as it had Betty and me. You become keenly aware of your need for fellowship with friends and neighbors. Even in the most modern environment, where people rarely know their neighbors, the need for human fellowship is vital at a time of sorrow.

Discussing this, I remembered a funeral that I attended several years ago. It was for a man whom I didn't really know, the stepfather of a friend. I attended because I thought there wouldn't be many people there; still, how few there were amazed me. No one was in the chapel that morning except his son and daughter-in-law, his widow, and his landlord. It was the saddest funeral I have ever attended. The widow was prostrate with grief and nobody cared.

The funerals of the three men our church had lost were so different! In each case the family leaned heavily upon God. In each case the comfort of friends and of the Holy Spirit was something I shall never forget.

15

You Can't "Out-give" God

SEVERAL YEARS AGO a fine Christian woman said to me, "You know, no matter how hard I try, I cannot 'out-give' God. It is my deepest desire to be useful in His kingdom; but the more I give of my time and talent, the more He blesses me. The longer my list of service becomes, the more He adds to the benefits I receive. I've tried for years to 'out-give' God and it never works."

Tremendous examples of this were shown to me a few days after Bob Covington's funeral. In my poor way I had been making an effort to help them. Shirley was so grateful and felt rather bad because she didn't know how she could repay me.

I told her that when she was ready to go to the Social Security office, I would go with her. On April 15 we made the trip across town. As we were waiting for someone to help get her claim started, it occurred to me that I should check with them about my own account.

Aware that I had been overpaid in 1969, I had no idea how to return the money. As I explained this to one of the employees, she told me that it was necessary for me to file a financial statement every year so they could determine whether or not I had been overpaid. Deadline for the report was April 15—that very day. Penalty for not filing on time was equal to one month's check.

This came as a complete surprise to me. I sat there dumbfounded as she filled out the proper forms, one for me and one for Linda. If I had not made any effort to help Shirley, I would have lost a month's income. Here we were in this office on the last day for filing the report! Surely a Mind far greater than mine had worked this out.

And Shirley was worried because she saw no way for me to be repaid? Saving me a month's income was exceptional pay for a few hours work! Only God could have repaid in that measure—shaken down and brimming over.

A few days later I was to reap another reward for Christian service—a reward not material but so much more satisfying that I have no words to describe the elation I felt.

At Barbara's wedding reception a cousin whom I rarely see, invited the girls, my sister Ethel, and me to dinner.

The girls left shortly after dinner. As a result, I stayed longer than I would have, had they been there. As Nondes, Ethel, and I settled down to a long talk, the conversation turned to my writing. I mentioned that Miami Dade Junior College was planning a writers' conference in a few weeks and urged them to attend with me. Both of them were interested in writing but had not submitted anything to a publisher. Neither of them made any commitment and the talk veered in another direction. I forgot the incident.

A few days later Ethel called me for more information about the conference. A glance at my notes told us that tomorrow was the final day to register, and the final day to submit manuscripts for the competition.

She was working the next day and couldn't go to the college. I told her that if she got her story in shape and brought it to my house on her way to work, I would take it down, submit it, and have her registered.

She sat up late that night to retype the manuscript. Early the next morning she brought it to me. After all the details were taken care of, I grimaced at the thought of spending several days attending classes with Ethel.

Many years ago we lived next door to one another, and it was misery all the time. Our personalities clashed almost every day, until we couldn't stand each other.

Long ago I realized that my dislike for her was stunting my Christian growth. Every time I took communion, I choked on Matthew 5:23-24, "Therefore if thou bring thy gift to the altar, and there rememberest that thy brother hath ought against thee; Leave there thy gift before the altar, and go thy way; first be reconciled to thy brother, and then come and offer thy gift."

For this reason, when she entered the hospital for surgery some years ago, I wrote a letter telling her that I was truly sorry about our differences. Over the years a feeling of tolerration grew between us, but I never really liked Ethel. Even though I declared that I wasn't, I suppose that I was still clutching the old hurts close to me.

Thinking about it, I didn't know if I could enjoy a large dose of her company. Mulling it over, I decided what was done was done. Now I know the Holy Spirit led me to tell her about the conference and to arrange for her registration because He had a marvelous plan for me! I myself had not been able to overcome my feeling of dislike for Ethel, but in Christ everything is possible.

Before the conference began, I quipped to the girls, "If Ethel's manuscript wins a prize and mine doesn't, I'll croak."

And Ethel won!

The conference began with a banquet in a downtown hotel. The hall was filled with elegantly dressed people. At the close of the meal the dignitaries were introduced, we had a speaker, then Philip Wylie presented awards for the winning manuscripts.

He was lavish with praise for the authors. He emphasized that the work of the nine winners (in three divisions) was better than anything he had written in his college days or for many years thereafter. Then he made the announcements. In the juvenile division, the first prize winner wasn't present. So he quickly went on to the second prize.

"'Little Sam—'"

Recognizing Ethel's manuscript, I interrupted him with an ear-splitting shriek! He had to wait until my noise subsided before he could announce the complete title and Ethel's name. She was completely speechless!! I was shrieking and clapping so hard that I broke a blood vessel in the palm of my hand, and it hurt for days.

It was the strangest moment of my life. I think that I had every intention of being jealous if she won and I didn't. But the Lord chose this way of healing all my dislike of her. I was even more excited than if the award had been mine. Ethel's success proved to me that writing "ran in our family." Even though I sold quite regularly, I could not overcome the feeling that I was fooling myself—that I really couldn't write because no one in my family ever wrote. Now, I had a fellow author in the family! What a discovery! We were aglow with the Holy Spirit that night!

On the way home, I told her, "If I had our ancestors by the shoulders, I would shake them. Probably some of them had a talent for writing too, but they never used it."

Three of the fruits of the Spirit are love, joy, and peace. They were abundantly evident that night. A quarrel that had begun eighteen years ago was completely healed. The old grudge was lifted, just as fog disappears when the sun shines. What a bright new world it was!

And this was less than three weeks from the night I almost shot myself!

The Spirit of God moves mysteriously in your life and mine! What's up ahead?

No matter how inadequate I am for the future, no matter how I blundered in the past, Christ always has the answer for my present need. The greatest thing about His answer is the knowledge that He tailors every happening just for me in an exciting way.

16

What Next?

THE CONFERENCE WAS OVER. Ethel had made a good contact
with an editor. It seemed likely that she would sell "Little
Sam" to be published as a children's book. One unusual thing
that happened to me at the conference was an encourage-
ment.

The women's editor of the Titusville paper sought me out
and introduced herself. Quin, my roommate from the conference in Lake Placid in January, had told her that I would
be there. We talked about Quin for a few moments—what a
dynamic personality she was and what a lot of faith she pos-
sessed.

Suddenly the editor said to me, "I don't have the faith that
Quin has, but I especially wanted to meet you because Quin
came back from Lake Placid all enthusiastic about you! She
told me about your husband's death, and she has a strange
feeling that God has marked you for success! I have been
looking forward to meeting someone that could impress
Quin that much."

I was speechless! Quin impressed with mousey old me?
Of course, if anything showed through my plain exterior, it
would have to be the Holy Spirit in me. There is nothing
about me that would impress anyone, much less an active
person like Quin, who meets all kinds of people in her work

every week! It was a grand feeling to know that Christ was putting a quality into my personality that impressed others!

I had picked up several good ideas at the conference and felt an urge to get away from home and write. Earlier in the year, I had signed up for a tour of Europe and a trip to the Passion Play in Oberammergau, Germany. At the time I decided to go, the tour seemed to be just what I needed to broaden my outlook and to inspire me to write. Now at the close of the conference, I was filled with so many ideas for writing that what I really wanted to do was get away to our cabin in the mountains for a few weeks to sort out my thoughts and put them down on paper. It was only six weeks until my trip to Europe, and I had planned to sew a new wardrobe to take with me. With this in mind, I realized that I could not possibly spend the time in the mountains and be ready for Europe.

For several days I wondered if the European trip was what I needed at that time. Would I be doing the best thing or merely fitting into a mold? Doesn't everyone want to go to Europe at one time or another? Was I really hoping to broaden my outlook, or just running away to forget my problems for three weeks? I could not think of spending the money to go if it did not fit in with God's plan for me. In all probability I would never again get a chance to go. If I decided to go, I wanted to make sure that it was the right thing for me to do. The rumblings in the back of my mind were raising questions about the advisability of this particular trip.

Prayerfully, I attended a meeting of the women who were going on the tour from Miami. The tour guide was a lively, interesting woman I had met when I worked in the schools. Every year she substituted as a teacher just enough days to pay for the trip to Europe. I called substitutes for absent teachers, and for years we joked about my helping her to pay for her trip when I called her to come in and work. How I wanted to go with her! It seemed the natural thing to do. I had listened eagerly to her stories about Europe and had always wanted to go too. Now was my chance!

Just the same, that little voice within kept saying, "You quit work to write. God will supply all the ideas you will ever need. Get busy and put them down on paper!"

As the evening progressed, we saw slides of Rubye's previous trips. The women who toured Europe with her already were enthusiastic and reminisced as each new slide flicked into position.

It sounded fascinating; but, although I knew it would be fun, I began to see it as an extension of the rush and pressure that I knew at home every day.

Since Lawrence died, there hadn't been a day that I wasn't pushed to get something done. Endless details that I had never even thought about before kept me constantly jumping from one thing to another: insurance forms and legal technicalities, income tax returns, automobile repairs, a dozen other things, and deadlines to meet all the time! Even if the trip would be all fun and sightseeing, it loomed in the future as more of the same hectic activity. Would rushing around Europe meeting exacting schedules and living at an extremely fast pace for three weeks really help me? The Holy Spirit does direct in definite ways, because He changed my mind completely. As much as I had looked forward to going, I became aware that this was not the time for Europe. I cancelled my tour and began preparations for a trip to the mountains.

17

The Need to Get Away

AFTER I MADE MY DECISION to go to the mountains, it took me about a week to get everything in order so I could leave. The car needed new tires. The next-door neighbor adjusted my brakes. The motor hummed along, never missing a beat; so I didn't take it to the service station to be checked. In our family, this had been unheard of! Lawrence always checked every detail before we took a trip. Try as I would, I could not remember what it was that he did to it before we left. Larry and Wayne, the boys from next door who were interested in Linda and Jeannie, checked my oil and put some goop in the radiator. The car was ready to go; I would just have to trust the Lord to get me there.

The day before I left, I had lunch with Betty Griffin; and we had a long talk. Her faith was something to behold. Of the three of us who recently had lost our husbands, she was left with the most financial resources. Besides being heavily insured, Elliott had been part owner of a small aviation business, Southwind. Without the slightest idea how to do so, she was going forward in faith to learn some of the basics of the business. Her fifteen-year-old son wanted to keep it so that he could take over his father's interest in a few years.

As the conversation progressed, she related many incidents that emphasized God's guidance. One of the strangest things was an insurance policy they never expected to collect. Betty had no idea why Elliott had bought it. The conditions of the policy excluded payment if he died while at the controls of a plane, assisting as copilot, or even simply occupying the jump seat, deadheading back from a trip. It was unthinkable that Elliott would die in the back seat of a plane. He almost never rode as a passenger. He always flew it. To him, the policy seemed almost worthless, but Someone had prompted him to take it. And, through God's providence, Betty collected on it. It is helping to take care of his family today.

Our discussion moved to our lack of interest in the cemetery. Neither of us had any inclination to go there to feel close to our husbands. Betty and I felt that the houses we lived in, the personal things the men had done to make it a home, were far more of a monument to them than the tombstone in the cemetery. Betty's concern was for her mother-in-law, who visited the grave almost daily and watered the ground with her tears. Nothing gave her comfort as she grieved for her only son. Betty's love for her was amazing. In the midst of her own problems of adjustment, Betty prayed for her mother-in-law and counseled with her, trying to help her overcome the feeling of hopelessness.

The comfort that Betty and her children shared was in Elliott's eternal life, in his victory over death. When one is sure of this, the main problem is adjustment to the absence —not grief for the loved one. Elliott indeed had received a promotion and is in a far better place, where sin and pain and unhappiness are not. In 2 Corinthians 7:10 we found help. When we allow God to use sorrow in our lives, it helps us turn away from sin and seek to live a better Christian life. We should never regret His sending it. But the sorrow of the man who is not a Christian is hopeless and deadly, for death reflects his eternal loss. How grateful we are for the saving grace of Jesus.

As we discussed our mutual problems, our cares were lightened by being shared.

The next morning I left at daybreak. Destination: Blue Ridge. My first attempt at turnpike driving was a little exciting. In the early dawn I took the crosstown expressway and picked up I-95. I knew that my navigating instinct was up and working when the toll plaza for Florida's turnpike loomed ahead. The morning hours passed and the miles disappeared behind me. The car was on its best behavior, and I began to wonder why I had been afraid to take a trip by myself.

I ate an early lunch, and it was only 12:30 when I began to see the exit signs for Gainesville, Florida. For about twenty-five miles now I had been feeling strangely exhilarated. A Presence filled the car; and although He didn't convey anything in particular to me, I felt lighthearted, an emotion I had not felt since Lawrence became sick. Somehow, even though there was no direct message, the Holy Spirit seemed to be assuring me that this trip was the right thing.

It was my intention to stay in the mountains for three weeks. I had traded my trip to Europe for a vacation in a shack on the riverbank, and I felt no remorse—only peace and a sense of well-being.

Suddenly I slowed the car and left the interstate turnpike. I knew I was halfway to the mountains, and I decided to phone Carol Gasche. If she wasn't home, I would drive on. If she was, I hoped that she might ask me to come chat with her for a few minutes. She was home and gave me directions to the house.

The Gasches were old friends. They had moved to Gainesville about a year ago. When they lived in Miami, we all had worked together in Sunday school. Bob was a superintendent of the entire Sunday school, I was primary department superintendent, and Carol was my pianist. Because she was so talented, she was my artist too. No matter what I wanted for a bulletin board, Carol produced it. Sometimes we collaborated on flannelgraph stories. I would write a story or devotional and give it to her. Then she painted large characters to illustrate it on the flannel board. The children loved it, and we had a grand creative time teaching primaries. It made me feel good just to think of seeing the Gasches again.

What an afternoon I spent! They brought in my bags and installed me in one of the bedrooms. We discussed everything—my writing, Carol's writing, their new church, the good times we had enjoyed at Trinity—and finally Bob touched a sore spot. I had no intention of doing it, but I blurted out the fact that I was no longer active in the Sunday school. I had a personality clash with someone and used Lawrence's death as an excuse to bow out gracefully.

In a very kind way Bob called me a hypocrite. I don't suppose there is anyone else in this world who could call me that without arousing my resentment. Bob was different. We had worked together for years, and I had never heard anything from him but the kindest praise for my ability. I knew that his compliments about my work extended far beyond anything I deserved. So if Bob said I was a hypocrite, I must be one!

On the highway the next morning I began to pray. As I turned the situation over and over before the Lord, I could see the futility of my actions. On I-75 in South Georgia, my dislike for that church member left me. I have had no ill feeling toward him since. The Holy Spirit was truly riding in my front seat. That morning, one by one, sneaky little grievances disappeared. The closer I got to the mountains, the more I felt cleansed and ready to listen to the things God had to say to me.

I had no idea what the future held for me, but I was finding out by my own experience that "God is able to make it up to you by giving you everything you need and more, so that there will not only be enough for your own needs, but plenty left over to give joyfully to others."*

*2 Corinthians 9:8, *Living Letters.*

18

Twice as Much for God

MY FEELING OF PEACE was unreal even to me. I left Miami
tired, loaded down with cares and grief. I was on my way to
the mountains, not to escape grief but to conquer it. I had
walked through a winding valley. I stood in the shadow of
Lawrence's death. I walked down the road of financial set-
tlements which I hated. I came to grips with holidays and
special occasions, alone even in a crowd. I battled Satan
when my grief took over and my resistance was at its lowest
ebb. And I had found God in every experience.

To live in the cabin by myself was the last part of our old
life that I had to conquer. We were at the cabin when the
end of our marriage began.

It was in the mountains that I heard those hated words
from the doctor, "If I were Mr. Salls, I would be on a plane
for Miami *tonight*."

The last time I saw the cabin was the day I rushed there
to get our clothes before I took him to the Atlanta airport.

Could I do it? Could I sleep in the bed we had shared,
and live by myself? Could I sit on our beach at the table he
had built, and write? Could I walk alone down the riverbank
to the rapids, and endure the feel of the cool rocks, hard and
smooth with age? Could I do these things and not die inside?
By myself, never! With Christ anything is possible!

Unlike many people who have lost someone close, I never

had a feeling that Lawrence's personal belongings were unbearable to me. After the experience I had of seeing him the night I put on his pajamas for warmth, I wore them every night, hoping for a similar experience. Though the pajamas acted as a "Linus blanket," I never saw him again.

Instead of wanting to get rid of everything that was his, I found myself taking comfort in things that he had used and loved. I hoped that it would be this way with the cabin.

Hardly anyone expected me to stay three weeks. In my purse was a key to a dear friend's cabin, in case I couldn't stay in my own. Even I was not sure that I could do it, but I had to try.

To sell the cabin would be like selling part of Lawrence, but to stay in it day and night all by myself was something entirely different. I had spent only one night in my life alone in a house. Lawrence had taken the girls camping about ten miles from our home. Then my neighbors were only seventy-five feet away.

On the mountainside, the summer cabins in our bend of the river would be closed this time of the year. This meant my nearest neighbor was over a mile away!

Yet, God did not give me a sense of fear but of peace and courage. There was a feeling of adventure inside me as I drove along the Interstate.

I was ninety-two miles south of Atlanta when the Spirit began to guide me contrary to my plans. It was my intention to drive several miles farther to a Holiday Inn for lunch. Instead I felt a strange urge to take an earlier exit. For a while I poked around in an outlet store, seeking nothing, really.

My eyes rested on a small plaque. I read the message there: "God grant me the serenity to accept the things I cannot change, courage to change the things I can, and wisdom to know the difference."

Now I had seen this prayer before. It was by no means new to me. Someone had even given Barbara a ceramic plaque with this prayer on it for a shower gift. Another friend admired it and told me how much the prayer had meant to her through the years. One of the things I did before I left was to look everywhere until I found a plaque with that prayer for her. But it didn't speak to *me*. Today in this wayside outlet store it was saying to *me*. "Your life is as God has ordered it. Take what you have and make the most of it."

Abruptly I was hungry and drove across the street to a truck stop before returning to the Interstate.

As I bowed my head for grace, my mind was preoccupied and I uttered a singsong, stereotyped little prayer: "Come, Lord Jesus, be our guest, and let these gifts to us be blessed. Amen." Before I finished lunch I felt a strange sensation. I knew that my prayer was answered and Christ was there as a guest at my table. I expected to see Lawrence again, as I did the night in my bathroom; but I didn't.

When I finished eating, I paid my bill and stepped through a door to the restroom. Apparently Christian people ran the restaurant, because there was a tract rack on my left. I selected one of each, thinking that God may have a message in one of them for me. But there was no message.

Instead, as I was washing my hands, a definite thought entered my head like a flash. It was not just the usual everyday things that I must do in Lawrence's place; it was also the godly mission that he had left undone. I had to do twice as much for the Lord, as if he had lived.

A big job! Now I would have to wait for orders from the "Commanding General."

Back on the Interstate the feeling that something big was

opening before me persisted. As the car sped towards Atlanta, ideas and encouragements kept popping into my head. Instead of being lonesome on the long ride, it was as if this were the first time I had separated myself from the world long enough to think and pray and listen for God's guidance.

Jeremiah 33:3 came to my mind. "Call unto me, and I will answer thee, and shew thee great and mighty things, which thou knowest not."

When my children were young, they called that God's telephone number. "If you are in doubt about just what to do, God's telephone number is Jeremiah 33:3," they said.

My mind dwelled on the widow's mite of Mark 12:41-44. Christ is not interested in *how much* you have to give, but it is important for us to give everything we have to Him. In other words, a poor struggling soul with little to offer who dedicates his all to Christ pleases Him more than a rich man with many abilities who simply tosses God some of his excess.

Surely the widows of today, emancipated by education and with insurance, have more to give than the widow of the Bible. But what? Just what is our function in life? Where can we invest our money and our talents to be most pleasing to God? How can we be sure what is God's will for our lives? We're a strange, restless army. Thousands of widows are groping for an answer. What does life mean, alone, without the spouse?

What does God expect?

My children were almost grown. Soon they wouldn't need me. Could I make something of my life, or must I sit on a shelf from now on?

I answered my own questions when I thought about obedience to His will. Ruth of the Old Testament was so poor a widow that she gleaned barley from the field of Boaz. It was a sort of welfare, I suppose; but that was her lot in life. She accepted it and worked diligently at it to take care of her aging mother-in-law, and her name and example have been known to succeeding generations! Not only that—she became the ancestor of our Lord Jesus Christ!

The important thing is to *listen* for His instructions and seek His will. Cannot the God who produces a huge tree from a mustard seed, produce in us great works if we grow in Him?

19

It Doesn't Look Encouraging

By three o'clock that afternoon I was on the outskirts of Atlanta where I planned to spend the night with Eva Lee and Bill Odom. We had met the Odom's while camping seven years ago. They have five sons and we have five daughters. With that combination it was inevitable that we remain friends.

They owned a cabin about five hundred feet up above the river from ours. I had called Bill and asked him to wire my cabin for electricity. He had put in the meter box and everything necessary to connect it, but there was no inside wiring.

My overnight visit stretched into two nights. They helped me find a small refrigerator; and Friday Bill took a day of his vacation and went to the mountains, my refrigerator in the back of his pickup truck.

Eva Lee rode in my car. Though she wouldn't try to talk me out of doing what I planned, she didn't believe that I could possibly manage. She had a heart of gold and had cleaned the cabin a few weeks before, carefully removing all of Lawrence's personal things. The closer we came to the river, the more nervous *she* was; and strangely enough, I was perfectly all right.

The mountains were lovely. I had come hoping to see the dogwood in bloom, and I was not disappointed. We could hear the river singing as it hurried over the rapids. Spring-

time in the Blue Ridge Mountains! If that didn't inspire me
and chase away my depression, nothing would.

We met my cousin walking on the mountain road, before
we came in sight of the cabin. He had bad news for me. The
carpenter I hired to build a sleeping porch and a room for my
bathtub had the lumber delivered, but the work was not even
begun.

That was a real disappointment! Talking to me on the
phone about four weeks ago, he had promised me it would be
done within a week. Two hundred and fifty dollars worth of
lumber was lying on the ground, warping in sun and rain.
My car was loaded with a chest of drawers and miscellaneous
items that I planned to put into the new addition.

The cabin, as it stood, was only eight by sixteen feet.
There was a bed and a chest of drawers at one end; and a
sink, a gas hot plate, and a tiny table at the other end. The
men unloaded my refrigerator and squeezed that into the
cabin too. Bill set to work installing two electric plugs, one
for the refrigerator and electric blanket, one for a light and
the electric clock.

I went up on the mountainside to see if I could hook up
our gravity-flow water system. I did all the things I could
remember to do—put the trough in the spring, set the tank
under the trough, and connected the plastic pipe to an opening in the tank. Theoretically, I should have had water in the
kitchen sink by the time I returned to the cabin. I didn't.
I traced the pipe from the cabin back to the tank. There were
no leaks. Neither were there any joints that I could get apart
to see where it was stopped up.

I've heard other widows say the hardest part of the adjustment was the realization that they had no male person to talk
to. That was not my biggest problem. I am outgoing enough
that people talk to me all the time. Lawrence was the quiet

type; he never had much to say. But he was always *doing* something for me, and I could *depend* on Lawrence to know everything about anything that needed to be done.

There I stood in the woods on the side of the mountain. The water system wouldn't work. I'd done everything I knew to do and had not the faintest idea what was wrong with it. I knew that Lawrence would have known what the trouble was, so I trudged up and down the line a few times trying to think what he would do. It was no use. My mind just did not run in the same channel. Almost in tears, I went to get Dale, my cousin, to help me. He and one of his visitors fixed it. Air in the pipe had been obstructing the flow. After the water was coming into the faucet, they tacked screens on the windows; and the cabin was as ready as it was going to be for a while. My only modern comforts were one light bulb, the electric blanket, the refrigerator, and cold water in the tap. The cabin was no bigger than a good sized tent.

And then it began to rain. It rained that night and the next day. Marguerite, Dale's wife, came over and begged me not to stay by myself. She could see that I intended to, so she threatened, "Betty, you won't be here a week until you will be kidnapped or raped."

Finally she made me promise that I wouldn't stay during the day when the carpenters were working on the building. She didn't want it to be common knowledge that I was alone. I had lunch with them, and they packed up and went back to Miami.

It rained that afternoon and quite a bit of the night. Sunday morning, when I tried to get my car up the hill to go to church, all it did was spin its wheels and slide into the ruts. In trying to back down, I ran it into the side of the mountain; and then I couldn't get it up or down. So I left it blocking the road. No one could come in or out until they moved my car. After lunch Bill and his father-in-law went up and brought it part way down and parked it in the entrance to an old lumber road no longer used.

They left and went back to Atlanta with many misgivings and after urging me to stay in their cabin because it was bigger and more comfortable. Now there was only one other cabin occupied in our bend of the river. I settled down to reading and writing. The rain came down harder and harder.

Just after dark, I heard the car motor start at the next cabin. The Safrits and their friends were leaving too. By now the road was so muddy I knew they must have had to put on chains before they left. They paused for a moment in front of my cabin; but it was pouring, and I didn't go out and they didn't come in. I waved them on. Slowly the lights disappeared in the woods. No neighbors for over a mile and no telephone! My car was unable to make it up the hill without chains (and I certainly have no idea how to put on a pair of chains), so the only way for me to get out was to walk! My only consolation was that no one was likely to come out in this rain to kidnap me. Could I stick it out; or would I have to give up and admit defeat, and perhaps sell the cabin?

20

No Bigger Than Fishermen

MONDAY MORNING the sun was shining. We have a standing joke here on the river. We're the only Presbyterian family; the rest are Baptists. It truly always rains when the Baptists are here. When we are here by ourselves, we never get more than a few sprinkles. One year we left for home at four o'clock in the morning with no inkling that there was a cloud in the sky. At 4:15 a rainstorm hit that threatened to wash the mountain away. Of course it was coincidence; but I teased my cousins, telling them that was Baptist weather. The Lord doesn't do that to Presbyterians because He knows we are afraid of water! It had worked for seven summers, and it was working my first day there by myself.

I felt no uneasiness. Surely as soon as the road dried off, I could get the car out.

At two o'clock I decided to try.

As I pulled it forward about fifty feet, it began to spin.

Then two fishermen rounded the curve. Actually they were probably normal-looking men, but in my mind's eye they were dark, grubby villains. I backed into the lumber road to let them pass. They waved and it scared me half to death. Everyone waves to you in the mountains, but I wasn't thinking about that. Out of sheer fear I flooded the engine, and it wouldn't start again. The fishermen were already past, and I didn't want them to know I couldn't drive out. I know how to "unflood" it under the hood; one of the elders in my church had taught me. So I got out to work on the car, forgetting to set the emergency brake. As I leaned on the front of it, it moved backward toward the river. Frantically I ran after it, jumped in, and slammed the brake to the floor! I made it! The car stopped so fast, it was rocking back and forth. I was rocking right with it. I could hardly catch my breath. Gingerly, I tried the engine; and it sprang into action.

But I was too tired even to try to get up the hill, I returned to the cabin, taking the "top road" so the fishermen wouldn't see me. I loaded the shotgun and sat down to wait. In about an hour they left, not knowing or caring that I was there by myself.

Around four o'clock I tried to drive the car up the hill again and failed. I decided to wait until morning; and if I still couldn't drive out, I would walk out and ask for help and stay in the Gooches' cabin on the main road for a few days. I ate my dinner and was quite content to stay there another night. When it was almost dark, I heard a jeep coming up the river road. It stopped in front of my house; and I recognized one of the two men, Jarrell Anderson from Blue Ridge. He had promised to come now and then to see if I was all right. And here he was.

I told him I couldn't get the car out.

He urged, "Betty, why don't you go stay in the Gooches' cabin? They want you to, and it would be a lot better for you."

Jarrell knew these mountains and the people in them just like he knew his own backyard. I asked him, "Jarrell, do you think that it's dangerous for me to stay here alone?"

"Weeelll," he said, "you may get sick, or you may fall down, or the car may not start. Why don't you stay at the Gooches'?"

"I'm not afraid of those things. I'm afraid of *people*. Do

you think that the fishermen who come to the river will hurt
me?"

"No-oo, but you may get sick, or you may fall down, or the
car may not start. Come on. I'll get your car out for you,
even if I have to pull it with the jeep. Why don't you stay
at the Gooches'?"

I knew that in about two more sentences I was going to
break into loud wailing sobs. What a horrible thing that
would have been to do to two men who only came to help!

So I said, "OK, I'll pack my bags."

They carried my typewriter, writing supplies, portable file,
clothes, and food to the jeep. Jarrell drove my car out with
no trouble at all. He rode those ridges as well as I drive on a
paved road. Allen, the man with him, drove the jeep; and we
went to his house so I could call the builder who was supposed to build my porch and bathroom. He promised to be
there on Saturday with enough men to get it done on the
weekend.

Then we went to the Gooches' cabin. Jarrell, just out of
the hospital and hardly able to be doing all this, carried my
things in, helped me find the lights, and then drove to the
top of the mountain to turn on the water. Nothing came out
of the spigot. At first we couldn't figure out why. Then I
heard water running under the house, and we realized that
Chug had disconnected and drained the pipes to avoid freez-
ing.

Jarrell went under the house and filled two buckets. Then
he had to go back to the top of the mountain to turn off the
water. By now it was after ten o'clock, and he promised to
come back the next day to connect the water.

Compared to my cabin this one was sheer luxury, even
without water. Large heaters warmed it, as I leisurely pre-

pared for bed. It was a different feeling, knowing that neighbors were only a few hundred feet away!

The last verse I remember reading in my Bible that night was Matthew 28:20 ending in these words: "and be sure of this—that I am with you always, even to the end of the world."*

I'm not sure whether I was awake or asleep; but in my semi-conscious mind, the Lord had a good talk with me that night: "If your God is no bigger than the fishermen on the river, why are you writing about faith? What could you possibly have to say that would be of any value? You might as well go back to Miami and dream up 'true confession' stories. Remember, My promise is that I will be with you always, even unto the end of the world. I'll be there, wherever you are."

I awoke the next morning, took my clothes and my typewriter, and started back to the cabin. First I stopped to let the McClains know where I was. Allen was the one who helped Jarrell last night, so I wanted to speak with them before I moved back. My conversation with them only strengthened my determination to stay in my own cabin.

Although I hadn't met the McClains before last night, they were a Miami couple, friends of my sister and brother-in-law, and had migrated to the northern Georgia mountains.

During our conversation they related how they came to buy their house, at the time a summer cabin. Everything worked out so well; it was just the Lord's will, they told me. As I thought about it, I remembered when their house stood vacant and for sale. Lawrence and I saw it before they did, and yet the Lord had not urged us in any way to buy that or any of the other land on the main road. By now the best lots in that area had been sold. But we had come here when

Living Gospels.

plenty of land was available. If the Lord meant for me to live on the main road, I believe He would have given us a little nudge, urging us to buy several years ago.

On the other hand, our own purchase had come about in such a way that it seemed God must have had His hand in that too. Back to the river and the woods for me!

I stayed there a week, venturing out occasionally to let people know that I was still looking for a carpenter. The man who had promised to come on the weekend said, "If you can find someone to do it sooner, do that."

It stayed dry, and my car trudged in and out without a complaint. Saturday passed and the carpenter didn't show up. The lumber was still lying on the ground. A neighbor from the main road did come on Sunday to pile it up on cement blocks, and he covered it with plastic. He was a builder, but he could not get to the work for at least a month. He promised to look for someone who could do it sooner.

Sunday evening I prayed with an open heart for God to let me know just what to do. "You know, God, that lumber is here and I have to pay for it. I can't very well return it after it has been lying there in the weather for four weeks. You know I can't afford to pay for something I can't use. If You think I should build, You will have to find a carpenter."

Monday, as I read my Bible, Isaiah 54, verse 2 sprang at me from the pages of the book. "Enlarge your house; build on additions; spread out your home!"*

I pondered this verse for quite a while and decided that, if I found a carpenter, I was going to build the cabin large and comfortable—no skimping along with a bathroom and a porch!

I was sitting on the beach almost at the waterline as I made the decision. The presence of the Holy Spirit became

Living Psalms and Proverbs.

very real and assuring. In my mind's eye I could see Lawrence standing behind me on the river bank.

"Go ahead and build it," he said. "It's what we've always wanted to do."

About two hours later a man came down the mountain road looking for work, and I hired him. He was the only carpenter I knew in the whole county, except the one that stood me up. This man had built the Odom's cabin and done a good job. He was the only man I wouldn't have been afraid to hire!

Completely forgetting my promise to Marguerite not to stay there while the carpenters worked, we began building a house the next day!

21

Push Back the Walls

YES, I AM THE VINE, you are the branches. Whoever believes in Me and I in him shall produce a large crop of fruit. For apart from me you can't do a thing."*

My "large crop of fruit" for the next few weeks was a house—three bedrooms, a bath, and a living room added to the original cabin. Mysteriously, the same day I found a carpenter, a bulldozer appeared and began to grade the mountain road. I hadn't even thought to pray for that; but before the week was out, all the ruts had disappeared and there was a new gravel top. This meant no more trouble getting out in wet weather. The same man who fixed the road also was able to install septic tanks. I hailed him in the woods one day and gave him my order, and it was accomplished.

Allen McClain came to work with Mr. Hooper, the carpenter; and they made a great pair. Things were happening so fast that I never had a chance to draw up even a rough plan to show them what I wanted.

I just went ahead of them and said, "Put a wall here and a window there!"

The building turned out so well that, when it was only half finished, a magazine editor I was corresponding with about another piece asked me to do an article on how to

*John 15:5, *Living Gospels.*

115

build a summer cabin. I managed to write that too, and it helped pay for the cabin.

During the weeks the men were there, I worked harder than I had ever worked. But then I had never built a house before. A new respect was born in me for construction workers. I watched them work, piece by piece, as they put the house together. They lifted and climbed and did everything but swing from the rafters. Of course I had seen houses built on the flat land of South Florida; but they were not *my* house, springing from the side of the mountain. I was intensely interested in every detail.

The lumber truck broke down and deliveries were delayed; so I began to haul lumber, windows, and bales of insulation in the car. The weather was dry, and we were racing to get the walls and roof together before it rained. I painted and one day found myself on the scaffold, painting the outside of the second story to rush the job along.

By myself, I couldn't have done that! I didn't dare look down. I just kept saying, "Now God, I started this house because You told me to. I'm sure You don't want me to fall off this thing. Just keep me topside if that's Your will."

I didn't have to stay up there long; but I found I could do it through Christ who strengthens me, and without Him I could do nothing.

Probably for someone else to plan that house and keep everything going would have been no problem. For me, it was a miracle. A year before I couldn't even turn on the dishwasher in my own kitchen. It hooked to the sink faucet; and every time I tried to connect it, it squirted me with water; so Lawrence or the girls always did it.

Hire the workers, haul the lumber, and paint on a scaffold? Never! But through Christ I did it.

When the building was almost finished, a message came

from the Spirit, that was so strong it woke me up out of a deep sleep.

"By the time Lawrence has been dead nine months (the same length of time you carried your children) you will have conquered your grief. The house will be completed, and your depression will wander off to a distant mountaintop, and you will be free to live a new life."

How could that be? The twenty-third of May, nine months from the day Lawrence died, was only a week away. Nevertheless, I sat up in bed and wrote down the message just as it came to me, so I wouldn't forget it.

Eagerly I looked forward to the twenty-third of May, expecting a miracle. Hadn't God already shown me that He "is able to do exceeding abundantly above all that we ask or think"?*

He works in mysterious ways. The only thing He gave me on the Saturday that I looked forward to so much was cabin fever. It started in the afternoon—a vague dissatisfaction.

Daily I had been adding to the clutter in the original cabin: a linoleum for the bathroom floor, curtains for the new windows, and hanging lamps for the living room—along with the large amount of books and writing supplies I had brought with me. The one room wasn't built to hold *any* of that.

The Odoms arrived from Atlanta with a truckload of furniture; and we spent the afternoon scrubbing, spray-painting, and refinishing. For the time being, the cabin would be furnished in "Early Miscellaneous"—revived castoffs and hand-me-downs.

Later in the evening I could feel the walls of the little room closing in on me. Although the night was cool, I was hot and restless. I turned first one way and then another, but

*Ephesians 3:20.

sleep evaded me. At seven o'clock I got up feeling nauseated.
When I went outside, I felt fine. When I came back in, I
felt miserable and shortwinded. I had an idea what was
wrong with me.

Once agan the Odoms helped me over a hump. There was
a stack of Sheetrock blocking the door between the old cabin
and the new addition. They helped me move that, and we
opened the door to connect the old and the new parts of the
house. Then I did a thorough job of housecleaning, storing
everything I could in the new part. After that I felt fine, but
I was disappointed. Was I mistaken? Was the message I
received in the night only a dream that meant nothing? No
great revelation had appeared to me nine months from the
day Lawrence died.

Two days later I began to arrange the furniture and make
up the beds upstairs. As I worked I realized in a flash just
what cabin fever meant. The sluggish, disinterested feeling
when I closeted myself in the old cabin represented the frus-
tration when I limited myself to my old life. I was to push
back the walls of my life just as we had enlarged the cabin.
The old cabin was just great, but it had its limitations. Now
I was eager to see it enlarged and filled.

The old life had been just great, but I had put many limitations on it by saying, "I can't."

Now I was to open my life and fill it. As I became miserable in the old cabin, so would I be miserable if I returned
to the shell of grief that I had worn for nine months. It was
time now to step out as an individual and accomplish greater
things for Christ. Misery can destroy you if you cling-to it.
Hope in Christ can fill your life and make you a new person.

The following Saturday I entertained my first guests for
dinner in the new house. Tom and Margaret Shippes, who
had faithfully trekked back here to see how I was, were de

lighted with the results of my efforts. As they went from room to room, examining every detail, my depression did wander off and sit on a distant mountaintop.

As the evening progressed, I realized that God did not miss His timing. He told me the house would be finished and my grief would subside in nine months, the same length of time I had carried my children. I never had a baby that wasn't at least a week late, so He was true to His word.

That night I found a sense of accomplishment that I never expected to experience in those first dark days when I became a widow.

By worldly standards, the house is not elegant; but it did turn out to be creative and functional. The linoleum on the living-room floor is covered with big red roses, a breach of decorating skill if I ever saw one! Everyone comments on my rose-covered floor.

The laughter it evokes, says to me, "Your life need not be dull."

22

A Living Monument

NINE MONTHS and ten days after my husband died, everything
did fit into a wonderful design. The house was finished, and
the plumbing was installed. Then for two days, it rained,
more rain than I have ever seen on the mountainside.

The creek rose, the river was high in its banks, and I was
filled with thankfulness that the house was warm and dry—
thankful that the Lord had held this deluge until the major
part of the building was over. I felt a little like the biblical
wise man who built his house upon the rock. Though the
rains came in torrents, and the floods rose, and the storm
winds beat against his house, it would not collapse, for it was
built upon a rock.*

Finally, my house as well as my spirits was in order. The
rain gave me no concern. The house was large now, compared to the tiny space I had when I arrived on the mountainside. My typewriter was set up by my bedroom window, fac-
ing the river. The meager furnishings had taken their places,
and I was comfortable. I had received word from my pastor
that he was planning to use the cabin for an overnight stop
with some teenagers on the way to a Bible conference in
Montreat. Already the Lord was using the house for His
purposes.

My writing was progressing nicely. God was answering

*Matthew 7:25.

my prayers in this area. He was supplying more ideas than I could find time to write.

At 8:30 that evening, through the rain I saw headlights and heard a horn on the river road. The Odoms had arrived for four days. He came to finish wiring the house. At last, there would be no more need for the maze of extension cords, and an electric stove would replace the hot plate I had been using. Almost two weeks had passed since they had seen the house, at that time lacking walls and roof. Joyfully I showed them through each room. It was exactly the plan that I had envisioned four years ago when we built the original cabin.

This was a living monument erected in Lawrence's memory, a place where all of us could come aside from the rush of living. The spot where the end of our marriage began, had come alive with a house instead of a primitive cabin. Working creatively in this place, in the midst of God's grandest handiwork, was far more meaningful to me than sitting, brooding, in the cemetery beside his grave.

Knowing that I had not been going out in the rain, the Odoms had brought the mail from my box on the main road. Joyous news! Shirley Covington was the mother of a redheaded, six-pound boy, Philip Andrew.

At first there had been complications, and she had to be rushed to the hospital in an ambulance. Fifteen more minutes and both the mother and the child might have perished! But, as we have already learned, God's will is to be. And His will was for Shirley to deliver a healthy boy. This was her monument to Bob, that God had accomplished through her in memory of him. To bear and rear his child—what a profoundly more satisfying accomplishment than to mope beside his grave!

As I read the letters, I thought to myself, nine months ago I lost my husband. At almost the same time, Bob Covington rededicated his life to Christ and joined the church, and Shirley conceived a son. In the ensuing time, both Elliott and Bob were taken. For three families life has changed radically. Even so, all is well; God is working in our lives.

I felt the power of God's love and guidance when I read a newspaper clipping in one of the letters. The article, "Column with a Heart" in the Miami Herald, contained a letter that Shirley had written in answer to one previously printed and signed "Bewildered." "Bewildered" had written, "How do people manage financially these days if they don't have a husband in the home? The emotional management is crucifying enough. The money management destroys too. Do others know this?"

She went on to say that her lovely home had no mortgage, and her $75,000 in insurance money was invested at seven percent; yet she and her children (ages twelve, fourteen, sixteen, and twenty) could not possibly make ends meet on the interest, the amount she received from Social Security, and her salary. She ended by saying, "Nine tenths of my life was destroyed when my husband died; the other tenth is being destroyed financially."

Shirley's answer was full of life and an inspiration to anyone in difficulty:

Dear Eleanor Hart:

My husband had been dead less than two weeks when the letter from "Bewildered," the worried widow with four children, appeared in your column.

It is much too soon for me to tell what or how much income I will have on which to live. All our debts are paid, except the mortgage of $15,000 on a $30,000 home, which I must assume. We will have to live on our income from Social Security and a small V.A. pension. There are no investments yielding interest, and I will not be able to work for the present.

You see, I am carrying a child, to be born within the next month. We have two sons, fourteen and nine, and by my husband's first wife, a daughter, twenty, who is self-supporting.

Devastating? No. If I were left with nothing but my faith in God, it would be enough. Only He is able to supply all our needs, physical and emotional. Already I have had clear evidence of His loving care through the genuine care and concern of friends and loved ones who are helping me in His name.

But more than material wealth, which my husband did not leave me, he left me with fifteen years of happy memories. We were utterly devoted to each other, and I would rather have had the fifteen happy years than fifty mediocre ones or even a quarter of a million dollars in the bank. Look for your blessings, *Bewildered,* and count them. There are other blessings than money: good health, a purpose for living, ability to work, and a sense of being productive and needed.

Faith in the Future

In prayer that night I felt assured that Betty Griffin's problems were being ironed out too. I knew that she would put her faith in God and go ahead. She would make the transition from a sheltered life to that of a widow and handle her affairs with confidence. Just as she had accepted Elliott's death in faith, so would she carry on her new life with the help of God. She would lean heavily on God as she made her decisions about what to do with her interest in Southwind. The thing she disliked most about the adjustments would be her greatest victory. In Christ she would find the answer: "But I will preserve your fatherless children who remain; and let your widows depend on Me."* Southwind and the library in San Juan will be Elliott's monuments.

*Jeremiah 49:11, *Living Psalms and Proverbs.*

The marble headstones we placed on the graves were meaningless. If a monument is going to help heal your grief, it must be a living tribute: a house that rings with laughter and praise, a library filled with information, or a son to grow in wisdom and grace. These are the things that are meaningful to the living. Indeed, our very lives must be a living monument to their memory. If the world is to profit from the deaths of these young men, the people of the world must be able to see Christ in us.

"For if we are faithful to the end, trusting God just as we did when we first became Christians, we will share in all that belongs to Christ. But *now* is the time. Never forget the warning, '*Today* if you hear God's voice speaking to you, do not harden your hearts against Him, as the people of Israel did when they rebelled against Him in the desert.' "*

The choice belongs to each of us. We can choose to follow on with Christ and receive His blessings, or we can choose to become bogged down in self-pity, mourning for what we have "lost."

God has set the pathway and He says, "Walk ye in it." It makes no difference what problem you face or how difficult your life has become. God is in command. You need only turn to Him in faith, believing, to find your answer! His promise is for everyone who will accept His divine guidance: "My grace is sufficient for thee: for my strength is made perfect in weakness."* *

We need our yesterdays. Whether they were good or bad, we gleaned wisdom and experience and knowledge from them. But in Christ, we never need be limited by what came before. Each day is a new beginning. Today is the first day of the rest of your life.

*Hebrews 3:14-15, *Living Letters.*
* *2 Corinthians 12:9.

Every day with Christ is exciting! There are valleys of depression, but *He is there*. The mountaintops beckon, and *He is there*.

"Seek ye first the kingdom of God, . . . and all these things shall be added unto you."† He has a plan for your life. No matter how insignificant or how important you are today, His plan will add a new dimension. New vistas constantly will open before you; there will be no dead end.

Eternal life and God's perfect plan belong to each of us who are His children through faith in Jesus Christ. You need only put your hand in His and say, "Yes, Lord, lead me on."

We can share in His riches only because He loves us so. He loved us in the beginning. He loved us even as His Son hung on the cross. He loves us right now. When we *abide* in this love, we will bear much fruit and our joy will be full.

My time is running out, but God's time is always in its proper perspective. He knows what is in store for me, because He planned it all—and there is no dead end.

†Matthew 6:33.